1
ORIGINAL STORY: TOSHIO SATOU
ART: HAJIME FUSEMACHI
CHARACTER DESIGN: NAO WATANUKI
Suppose a Kid from the LAST DUNGEON BOONIES Moved to a Starter Town

CONTENTS

CASE 1
That Day Was Like the Arrival of a Really Well-Mannered Super-Typhoon
003

CASE 2
That Encounter Was Like a God Came in on a White Horse
063

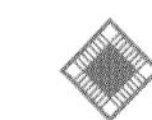

CASE 3
This Stroke of Luck Was Like Finding a Wish-Granting Magic Flower Growing in Your Backyard
121

CASE 4
This Shock Was Like Seeing a Jewel That Could Save the Realm's Economy Flung into the Ocean
155

VOLUME ONE

Original Story ◆ Toshio Satou
Art ◆ Hajime Fusemachi
Character Design ◆ Nao Watanuki

HERE, IN THE PEACEFUL VILLAGE OF KUNLUN, OUR STORY BEGINS.
IT'S TOO MUCH FOR YOU, LLOYD!
SCOLD
YOU TELL 'IM TOO, CHIEF!
SCOLD
SO THE WEAKLING OF OUR VILLAGE ...
...WISHES TO BE A SOLDIER IN THE CAPITAL, HMM...?
...YOUR MIND'S MADE UP, IS IT, LLOYD?
Y—
YES!
THERE ...
...WE FIND A BOY WITH HIS HEART SET ON BIDDING FAREWELL TO HIS HOME.

CASE 1
That Day Was Like the Arrival of a Really Well-Mannered Super-Typhoon

KUNLUN
THE SCENE NOW CHANGES TO THE AZAMI KINGDOM, OUR NEW STAGE.
KINDA FAR!
SIX-DAY TRIP
AZAMI KINGDOM
IT LIES ON THE SOUTHERN TIP OF THE CONTINENT UPON WHICH KUNLUN IS ALSO LOCATED.

AND IT IS IN THIS PROSPEROUS METROPOLIS...
WOW ...!
HUSTLE BUSTLE
CHATTER
LOOK AT ALL THESE PEOPLE! THE CAPITAL SURE IS SOMETHING ELSE...!
CLAMOR
BUZZ
...THAT THE BOY FIRST SETS FOOT.
CHATTER
KUNLUN VILLAGE BOY
LLOYD BELLADONNA

HIS FEET CARRY HIM TO THE CAPITAL'S EAST SIDE...
EAST SIDE
N
E
S
W
...A CHAOTIC, LAWLESS DISTRICT WHERE THE DREGS OF SOCIETY GATHER.

THE BULK OF THE RESIDENTS ARE MIDDLE- OR WORKING-CLASS FAMILIES, BUT HEAD FARTHER IN...
...AND IT'S A DIFFERENT WORLD, WHERE ALL KINDS OF FOLKS LIVE BY THEIR OWN RULES.
TASTY KEBABS HERE! HOT OFF THE GRILL!
OH! I'LL TAKE ONE!
YIPPEE!
YAY!
......
STARE

ACK!
NO! NO! GET IT TOGETH-ER.
DON'T GET SIDE-TRACKED!
SLAP
SLAP
I CAN'T BETRAY THE CHIEF'S HARD-EARNED TRUST...
—VERY WELL, LLOYD...

I'LL ALLOW YOU TO HEAD TO THE CAPITAL TO SEEK OUT YOUR DREAM OF BECOMING A SOLDIER.
TAKE THIS CRYSTAL BALL WITH YOU.

ONCE YOU REACH THE CAPITAL, SHOW THIS TO THE WITCH OF THE EAST SIDE.
SHE'LL COME TO YOUR AID... SHE'S A STUDENT OF MINE.
THE CHIEF'S SO AMAZING...
DREW HIM A MAP, TO BOOT

SHE EVEN HAS STU-DENTS HERE ...?
GUESS YOU GET AROUND IF YOU'RE OVER A HUNDRED!
TROT
TROT
TROT
THOUGH THE CHIEF OF LLOYD'S VILLAGE HAS THE APPEARANCE OF A LITTLE GIRL, SHE IS WHAT IS KNOWN AS A "LOLI GRANDMA."
WHO YOU CALLIN' A GRANDMA ...?!
...IS THIS IT?

THE WITCH OF THE EAST SIDE'S PLACE...

KRIK
KRIK...
WE GOT MEDS! —MARIE THE WITCH

...UM, EXCUSE ME!
CREEEAK...

!
FLIP
GLANCE
......
THE WITCH OF THE EAST SIDE
MARIE

FLIP
FLIP
WHAT DO YOU WANT?
OH...
WELL, I WAS TOLD TO COME HERE...
OHH? YOU BEAR A MES-SAGE?
NO... I'M NOT A MES-SENGER ...
THEN YOU'VE COME HERE AS A CUSTOMER SEEKING A WITCH.
THWAP

WERE YOU AWARE? SINCE ANCIENT TIMES...
...WITCHES HAVE DEMANDED PAYMENT OF EQUAL VALUE BEFORE GRANTING ANY WISH.
PAY-MENT ...?

YES.
YOU MUST BE PREPARED TO MAKE A SUITABLE SACRIFICE!

KNOWING THAT, WHAT WISH DO YOU DESIRE OF ME?
BADUMP
SACRI-FI...?
WISH ...?
BADUMP
INDEED.
BADUMP

ENSURE YOU DON'T REGRET YOUR CHOICE.
DOOM

I...
GULP

I'VE COME FROM THE BOONIES TO BE A SOLDIER!
I'D BE MUCH OBLIGED IF YOU'D LET ME STAY HERE A LITTLE WHILE!
ROAR!!

......
......
HUH?

UHH... ...A SOLDIER...
BABUMP
BABUMP
BABUMP
OBLIGED TO A WITCH...
......

AHEM! SINCE ANCIENT TIMES...
OH, YOU SAID THAT ALREADY.
JUMP
THEN GO FIND AN INN! THERE ARE ADS IN THE SQUARE!!
DAMMIT!!
THUD
CRASH

SHOCK
WHO GETS WITCHES AND INNS CONFUSED ANYWAY?!
IS THAT WHAT THEY TOLD YOU BACK HOME? WHERE ARE YOU FROM?!
AH!
UUU!
ARRRGH!
JAB JAB
UM...
KUNLUN...

UH-HUH.
WHEN YOU GO HOME, TELL THEM WITCHES AREN'T......
WHUMP
MM?
WAIT...
KUN-LU... N...
SHUDDER...

HEY, KID...
BY THE BY...
WHAT'S YOUR CHIEF'S NAME ...?
HUH?

HER NAME'S ALKA.
ビ
CRASH
?

MUTTER
NO, COULD JUST BE THE SAME NAME...
SWEAT SWEAT
MUTTER
AFTER ALL THIS TIME, I MEAN...
OH YEAH!
SHE SAID TO SHOW YOU THIS!

CLNK...
CHIEF ALKA'S CRYSTAL BALL!
ALL HOPE IS LOST! IT'S DEFINITELY HER!

SORRY, WHERE ARE MY MANNERS?! I'LL GET THE COFFEE BREWING ...!
WHIP
ZIP
FWIP
WHAT A FUNNY LADY...
GLOW

SO WILL THE CHIEF BE JOINING Y—
FLASH
!!
FWOOOM
TH-THAT LIGHT...!
FWOOOOSH
MISS WITCH, SEE FOR YOURSELF! THIS IS THE...
WHERE'D SHE GO ...?

LONG TIME NO SEE, MARIE!
SHIMMER
KUNLUN VILLAGE CHIEF
ALKA
PLEASE SHOW ME MERCY PLEASE SHOW ME MERCY PLEASE SHOW ME MERCY...

IT'S ME, YOUR MASTER, ALKA!
RING A BELL?
EEEEP!
SHE'S ON HER HANDS AND KNEES...
...

I HATE TO ASK A FAVOR AFTER ALL THESE YEARS...
GLANCE
BUT THIS PRECIOUS, DARLING VILLAGE BOY, LLOYD...
...HAS DECIDED TO BECOME A SOLDIER OF THE REALM.

UNTIL HE PASSES THE RECRUIT-MENT TEST...
...I HOPE YOU'LL LOOK AFTER HIM FOR ME.
......
CLUTCH

EEEP...... I-IF I MAY BE SO BOLD, I SHOULD LIKE TO ASK Y—
OH, BY THE WAY, I CAN'T ANSWER ANY QUESTIONS.

THIS IS MERELY A RECORD-ING!
APOLOGIES!
WHAP
SLAP
SLAP
SLAP
SLAP
SLAP
HEH HEEEH!
YOU REALLY HAD ME GOING THERE, PIP-SQUEAK!

I KNEW YOU'D SLIP UP IF I SAID THAT!
SPLAT
YOU'RE SUCH A SUCKER, MARIE!
EEEEP!
NOW SHE'S FLAT ON HER FACE...

KIDDING ASIDE, I DO WANT YOUR HELP HERE.
EVEN IF HE FAILS THE TEST...
GLARE

...I'M SURE YOU CAN PULL A FEW STRINGS FOR HIM.
EH, MARIE?
KH......

MMKAY! BUH-BYE!
AND LLOYD...
...IF YOU EVER GET LONELY, I'D BE HAPPY TO BE YOUR BEDFELLOW ANYTIME!
HISSSSSSS
!
SAY WHAT ...?!

TALK ABOUT EMBARRASSING, SHEESH...
HISSSS
STAGGER

SWISH
FWIP
......
BRUSH
BRUSH
BRUSH

PAT
......
PAT
PAT

CLICK
WHEW...

THWAM
DAMN HER TO HELL!!

BANG
I THOUGHT I WAS FINALLY FREE!
NOW I GOTTA HANDLE YOUR WEIRD FAVORS ?!
YOU DAMN LOLI GRAND-MAAA!
LOLI!
GRAND!
MAAAA!!
SLAM
WHACK
KICK
STOMP
BANG
HFF!
HFF!
UHH...

I FEEL LIKE I OUGHT TO APOLOGIZE FOR BRINGING ALL THIS ON YOU OUT OF THE BLUE...
OH...

FROM THE GET-GO, EVERYONE TRIED TO STOP ME COMING HERE.
THEY SAID SOMEONE LIKE ME COULD NEVER BE A SOLDIER...

BUT MY MIND'S MADE UP!
I'LL DO MY BEST TO NOT BE A BURDEN, SO PLEASE ...!

UM...
......

...WELL...
...IF IT'S HER ASKING, I DON'T HAVE A CHOICE.
I'LL LOOK AFTER YOU TILL THE TEST.
SO TO MAKE IT FORMAL...
I'M MARIE, THE WITCH OF THE EAST SIDE.
AND YOUR NAME IS...?
OH!
I'M LLOYD BELLA-DONNA.
UM, IF THERE'S ANYTHING I CAN DO TO HELP, I'D BE MORE THAN HAPPY TO...

NO NEED TO BE SO HUMBLE.
YOU CAN TAKE THE EMPTY ROOM IN BACK.
LEAVE YOUR THINGS THERE.
O-OKAY!

THUD
TAK
TAK
TAK

SPIN
?

THANKS FOR EVERY-THING!

BOW

!

FWIP

TAK
TAK
TAK...

......

HAAAH...
KUNLUN, HUH...?
CREAK

HE SEEMS A LOT NICER THAN THAT LOLI GRANDMA.
SIP
...WHAT A SUR-PRISE.

BY THE WAY!
SLAM
DON'T YOU DARE LAY A FINGER ON MY DARLING BOY, HOWEVER GOOD AND SWEET HE MAY BE!
POP
BFFT!
SPLOOOSH

TRY IT, AND YOU'LL SPEND THE REST OF YOUR LIFE AS A FROG!
TH-TH-TH- THE REAL ONE?! HOW ...?!

TELE-PORT SPELL!
USES THIS CRYSTAL AS A GATE...
PLEASE STOP USING MAGIC OUTSIDE THE REALM OF HUMAN ABILITY WILLY-NILLY!!

NO WAY WOULD I GO AFTER A KID I'VE ONLY JUST MET!
WHAT DO YOU TAKE ME FOR?!

PLAYING THE INNOCENT, ARE WE?
DIDN'T YOU RECENTLY SPEND HOURS DITHERING OUTSIDE A HOST CLUB DOWNTOWN...
...NEVER WORKING UP THE NERVE TO GO IN?!
YOU HAVE "VIRGIN" WRITTEN ALL OVER YOU.
I AIN'T NO V—
WAIT, JUST HOW MUCH DO YOU KNOW?!
HEY THERE!
ESCAPE!

ARE YOU SPYING ON ME?!
DOES THAT MEAN YOU SEE EVERY-THING THAT GOES ON HERE?!
HOH! HOH! HOH!
YOU DO?!

WELL ...!
I'LL AT LEAST GIVE YOU CREDIT FOR STOPPING YOURSELF.

IT SEEMS YOU HAVEN'T ENTIRELY FORGOTTEN YOUR POSITION.
THAT'S WHY I'LL TRUST YOU WITH HIM.
......

ONCE AGAIN, YOU HAVE MY THANKS ...
...MARIE.
......HAPPY TO HELP.
HMPH!
FREAKIN' LOLI GRANDMA...
SHUFFLE
RUSTLE

OH, AND ONE MORE THING...
YOU'VE CALLED ME A "LOLI GRANDMA" SEVERAL TIMES TODAY.
JOLT
HUH ?!
YOU KNOW ABOUT THAT TOO ...?!

AS PUNISHMENT, I'VE PLACED A MINOR CURSE OF MISFORTUNE ON YOU...
...IN ANCIENT RUNES.
BUH-BYYYYE!
THUD
YOU DID WHAAAT ?!!

WHAT SORT OF MIS-FORTUNES EXACTLY ...?
STUB
MY TOE ...!
HEH HEH!
THIS MUST BE-IIIIT!!
SLAM
AUGH ... D...

DAMN HERRRR!!!
THAT LOLI HAG... USING THE WISDOM OF THE ANCIENTS...
...FOR SUCH A PETTY GRIEVANCE?!
SHOOP
THE POWER OF RUNES COULD DESTROY THE VERY WORLD ...!
IT'S THE OLDEST FORM OF MAGIC THERE IS!!

RUNES REQUIRE IMMENSE RAW POWER AND SKILL!
IT TOOK ME THREE YEARS JUST TO LEARN THE "DISENCHANT" RUNE...
HOW CAN SHE JUST USE THEM LIKE NOTHING?!
TEAR
BAM

ON SUCH... PALTRY MISFOR-TUNES...
RUINING A SLEEVE AND THE LIKE...
DANGLE
SNAG
......

TALK ABOUT AN UTTER WASTE!!
WAAAH!
SHE HASN'T CHANGED AT AAAAALL!

DAMN HER! DAMN HER! DAMN HERRR!

TWEET
TWEET
ZZZ...
PEEP
PEEP
CHIRP
CHIRP
CHIRP
HNGH...
MMPH...
MM?!
TOK
TOK
TOK...

TOK
TOK
TOK
TOK
TOK
TOK
TOK
OHH...

I FELL ASLEEP HERE?
CREAK
SLIP...

!
AUGH...!
A BLAN-KET...?

HI!
GOOD MORNING!
SORRY TO TAKE OVER YOUR KITCHEN LIKE THIS.

I DON'T MIND... BUT ABOUT THIS...
OH, THAT WAS IN THE ROOM YOU GAVE ME.

HE PUT IT OVER ME...?
THANKS.
TOK TOK TOK...
TO BE HONEST, I'D WANTED TO CARRY YOU TO YOUR ROOM, BUT...

...I DIDN'T FEEL RIGHT ABOUT GOING INTO A LADY'S QUARTERS WITHOUT PERMISSION.

THANK GOODNESS HE DIDN'T SEE THAT...
MARIE'S ROOM
MESSSSY
SUCH A GENTLE-MAN...
IT'LL JUST BE A MOMENT.
I'M GRILLING THE PANCAKES NOW.
FLIP
TNKooo
HERE YOU GO.
SORRY I CAN'T MAKE ANYTHING FANCIER.
...NOT AT ALL.

—KEEP THIS UP, AND YOU CAN STAY HERE AS LONG AS YOU LIKE.
HUH?
NEVER MIND.
TIME TO DIG IN!
ADD A LITTLE DRIZZLE OF HONEY, AND...
BADUMP
BADUMP
CHOMP
MM!
THAT'S SOOOO GOOD!
WHEW...
SQUIK
CLATTER
......

I CAN SEE WHY MY MASTER DOTES ON HIM.
NOT THE MOST CONFIDENT, BUT SUCH A SWEET HOMEBODY OF A KID.
TOTALLY HER TYPE...
SIP
HE'S LIKE THE PERFECT HOUSEWIFE... AND LEAGUES AWAY FROM A SOLDIER HEADING TO THE FRONT...

...HM?
LLOYD, DO YOU REALLY WANT TO BE A SOLDIER?
WHAP
ばっ
OH! YES. SORRY.
NO, NO. THAT DOESN'T CALL FOR AN APOLOGY...

...EVERYONE TRIED TO STOP ME COMING HERE. THEY SAID SOMEONE LIKE ME COULD NEVER BE A SOLDIER...
......

YEAH... IT'S WEIRD, RIGHT?
HUH?! NO, NOT...
SPLOSH

I'M THE WEAKEST KID IN THE WHOLE VILLAGE.
I'M NO GOOD AT GATHERING FIREWOOD OR FISHING...
IF I SPAR WITH ANYONE, I'M SO HOPELESS, IT'LL TAKE ME A WHOLE DAY IN BED TO RECOVER.
TO A WEAKLING LIKE ME...
...THE SOLDIERS IN NOVELS, WITH THEIR STRENGTH AND HEROISM, ARE VERY ADMIRABLE.
......
I DON'T WANT TO GIVE UP ON MY DREAMS!
AT THE VERY LEAST, I HAVE TO TRY!

...I SEE.
AND I WILL!

THE GENERAL ADMISSIONS EXAM FOR THE AZAMI MILITARY ACADEMY...
CLINK
...THE ONE YOU'LL BE TAKING... IT'S NOT TILL THE MIDDLE OF THE MONTH, SO YOU STILL HAVE SOME TIME.

YOU KNOW WHAT IT ENTAILS?
A COMBAT TEST, A WRITTEN MAGIC TEST...
...AND AN INTER-VIEW.
THAT'S ALL I KNOW OF.

THE COMBAT TEST IS BY FAR THE MOST IMPORTANT.
SIP
I WAS AFRAID OF THAT.

THE MOST BASIC WORK OF A SOLDIER LARGELY INVOLVES SECURITY AND PHYSICAL LABOR.
YOU NEED TO BE STRONG.
UGH.

LATELY, COLONEL MERTHOPHAN, THE MAN IN CHARGE, IS REALLY GOING FOR IT.
HE'S RECRUITING ALL OVER AND SO ON. ...THE COMPETITION WILL BE FIERCE.
THOUGH WORD OF THEM MAY NOT HAVE REACHED YOUR VILLAGE...
...SOME OF THOSE RECRUITS ARE HOUSEHOLD NAMES AROUND THESE PARTS.
THE RUMORED "BELT PRINCESS," AMONG OTHERS...
HUH... YOU SURE KNOW A LOT.

I RUN A GENERAL STORE, SO I DEAL IN A LITTLE BIT OF EVERYTHING.
AND MOST PEOPLE ON THE EAST SIDE DON'T HAVE ANY MONEY...

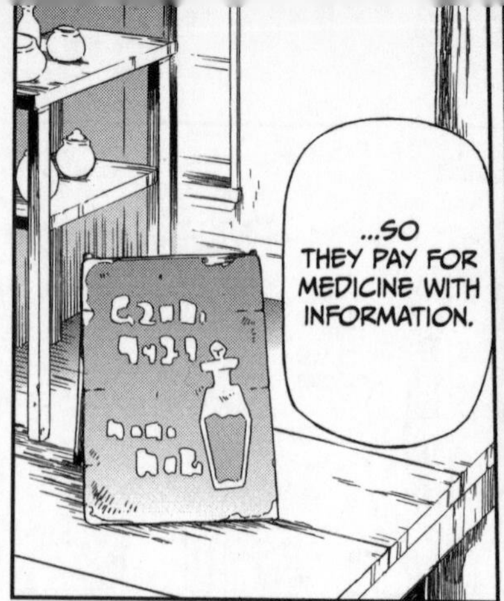
...SO THEY PAY FOR MEDICINE WITH INFORMATION.

URGH...
I WAS AFRAID IT WOULD BE ALL ABOUT POWER...

I'VE GOT ENTHUSIASM, BUT I LACK CONFIDENCE...
AND I'VE ALWAYS BEEN WEAK... WHY, EVEN ON THE WAY TO THIS LAND...
OH? YOU RUN INTO TROUBLE...?

YOUR VILLAGE IS ON THE FAR END OF THE CONTINENT.
MAKING IT ALL THE WAY SOUTH TO US IS A LENGTHY JOURNEY INVOLVING CONNECTING TRAINS AND WAGONS.
NOD NOD

YEAH, WELL...
AH... I SUPPOSE THAT'S NOT A SHOCKER.

THERE ARE EVEN DANGEROUS MONSTERS LURKING ALONG THE WAY.
SAY... HOW LONG DID IT TAKE YOU TO GET HERE?
OH!
UM...

SIX WHOLE DAYS......
IS THAT RIGHT...?
I SUPPOSE THAT'S DOABLE IF YOU TIME THE CONNECTIONS WELL...BUT YOU MUST'VE BEEN EXHAUSTED...
GULP GULP
OH! NO.

I RAN THE WHOLE WAY, AND IT STILL TOOK ME SIX DAYS!
ZIP
ZIP
ZIP
ZWOOP
YOU RAN ...?!
YESTERDAY
BFFT!

IT WOULD NORMALLY TAKE WAY LESS, HUH?!
NO, NO, NO!
BAM
YOU RAN ALL THE WAY HERE IN SIX DAYS?!
OH! YES. I RAN STRAIGHT HERE FROM HOME, NON-STOP.
KUNLUN VILLAGE (OUTSIDE MAP)
MAP OF THE CONTINENT
CROSS-CONTINENT
THIS KINGDOM
BABAM
YOUR ENDURANCE IS NUTS! NOT TO MENTION YOU'RE ABSURDLY FAST!!

BUT THEY SAID A VILLAGE GRANDPA COULD DO IT IN TWO DAYS.
OH, I THINK THEY MEANT WHEN HE WAS YOUNGER, BUT...
TRIP
TWO ...?!
THUD
ER, UH... LLOYD...
I KNOW BETTER THAN ANYONE HOW WEAK I AM.
BADUM DUM
DUM DUM
IS HE JOKING?! NO...
DUM
DUM

THAT FACE SAYS HE MEANS IT!!
LLOYD!
A HALF-BAKED KID LIKE YOU A SOLDIER?! YOU CAN'T EVEN FISH OR GATHER FIREWOOD RIGHT!
!
EVERYONE BACK HOME SAYS SO...
FLASHBACK: KUNLUN VILLAGE
YOU'LL NEVER MAKE IT IN THE MILITARY!
BUT ...
LISTEN UP, LLOYD.

THE ONLY WAY TO GET WOOD FROM A TREANT...
...IS TO KILL IT IN ONE HIT BEFORE IT DETECTS YOU! AND YOU CAN'T EVEN DO THAT!
KUNLUN VILLAGE LUMBER SOURCE
TREANT
SWING
SWING
THESE THINGS

TREANTS...
......
TREANTS ARE MONSTERS SHAPED LIKE TREES!
TERRIFYING CREATURES THAT ATTACK ALL HUMANS WHO DRAW NEAR...
IF YOU DEFEAT THEM ONCE THEY SEE YOU, THEY JUST VANISH.
DEATH
AND THAT'S NOT ALL.

"YOU'RE SO WEAK, WHEN YOU GO FISHING...
"...YOU STRUGGLE WITH A FEW FANGS AND HORNS!"
...THEY SAY!
KUNLUN VILLAGE FOOD SOURCE
KILLER PIRANHA
CAN SWALLOW A COW WHOLE
FISH?! THAT'S A MON-STER TOO!
"JUST BECAUSE YOU BROKE EVERY BONE IN YOUR BODY SPARRING...
"...IS NO EXCUSE TO SPEND A WHOLE DAY IN BED RECOVER-ING!"
...THEY SAY!
COMPOUND FRACTURES
ONE DAY
HEAL IN THREE HOURS, MAX.
IT ONLY TAKES YOU A DAY?!
HEY, ARE YOU SURE YOU'RE WEAK?!
SOUNDS MORE LIKE EVERYONE ELSE IS OUTTA THIS W...
I AM!
EVEN ON MY WAY HERE...

...I GOT VERY LUCKY AND ONLY ENCOUNTERED A FEW WILD ANIMALS.
IF I'D RUN INTO ANY MONSTERS, I'D'VE NEVER MADE IT!
I DID MEET...
...SOME LOCUSTS AND LIZARDS, THOUGH.
SO SCARY...
UH, THOSE ARE MON-STERS TOO!!
YOU DID RUN INTO THEM!

AREN'T MONSTERS MORE LIKE ...
..."THIS WORLD IS MIIINE!" ...?
PRETTY SURE THAT'S A DEMON LORD ...!
AUGH, GEEZ! LLOYD, YOU'RE REALLY STRONG!!
OH! THANK YOU FOR YOUR ENCOUR-AGEMENT...
SNIFF...
HAVE YOU NO CONFI-DENCE ?!

EVERYONE WAS WORRIED ABOUT ME LIVING HERE TOO, BUT...
...I TOLD THEM THE FISH EATEN IN THE CAPITAL DON'T HAVE FANGS OR HORNS ACCORDING TO MY NOVELS...
...AND THEY FINALLY RELENTED.
I TOLD THEM IT'D BE FINE.
NOVELS ...
I KNOW I'M WEAK...
...BUT I REALLY WANT TO BE A SOLDIER!!
THANKS FOR HELPING ME OUT!
CLENCH
SHE FOISTED A TOTAL MONSTER ON ME...
EEEEEEEAGHH! THAT LOLI GRANDMAAAA!
SHE'S UNBELIEV-ABLE!
I WISH I HAD SOME SKILLS TO HELP WITH THE TEST...
...BUT I'M ONLY GOOD AT HOUSEWORK, CLEANING, AND THE LIKE.
CLEANING?! AS IN... DISPOSING OF ENEMIES?!
TWITCH
HUH?! NO, NO!

GLEAM
GLEAM
GLEAM
JUST NORMAL CLEANING.
BUT...JUST YESTER-DAY...

...THIS KITCHEN WAS...
I GAVE IT A QUICK ONCE-OVER BEFORE I BEGAN COOKING.
FROM THAT TRAVESTY TO THIS ...?!
UM... YES... SHOULD I NOT HAVE?
HEH!

IT'S AMAZ-ING.
YOUR NORMAL CLEANING IS AMAZ-ING!
!
OH, IT'S NOTHING SPECIAL.
FOR A TOTAL BEAST...
EH HEH HEH...

...HE'S SUCH A NICE KID WITH A TALENT FOR BORING, EVERYDAY STUFF.
UM...!
YOU SEE, THERE'S A BIT OF A TRICK TO IT.
OH? WHAT HOUSE-HOLD WISDOM DO YOU HAVE FOR ME?
YES, YOU MIGHT CALL IT THAT.
SEE THIS RAG ...?
MM-HMM...

WIIIIIIPE...
SLAM
WITH AN ANCIENT RUNE ON IT, IT'LL CLEAN IN A SINGLE WIPE!
SEE?
THE DIRT JUST FALLS RIGHT OFF!
I'M SORRY! I FORGOT TO WIPE DOWN THE TABLE LEGS!

HOUSEHOLD WISDOM, MY BUTT!!!
HISSSSS
DID I DO SOMETHING BAD, AFTER ALL?!
NO ONE ELSE CAN DO THAT!

NO!
NOT BAD!
EXCEPT THAT IT IS!!
THE WISDOM OF THE ANCIENTS REDUCED TO HOUSEHOLD CHORES ...!
SLAM
SLAM
SLAM
?
?!
WHAT'S MORE, THAT'S THE DISENCHANT RUNE!
I SPENT YEARS SLAVING UNDER HER...
...JUST TO LEARN THAT THING!
WHAM
WHAM
FOR SOME REASON, IT GETS RID OF DIRT AND GRIME AS A SIDE EFFECT!
"FOR SOME REASON"?! (IT'S THE DISENCHANT RUNE, FOR CRYING OUT LOUD!)
WHAM
CRACK CRACK
WHAM
I'M SORRY. I KNOW IT'S NOT ANYTHING SPECIAL.
IT'S SO SPECIAL, IT HURTS!
WHAM
OH... THANK YOU VERY MUCH FOR BEING SO NICE... AGAIN.
I'M NOT TRYING TO CHEER YOU UP! BELIEVE IN YOURSELF A LITTLE, WOULD YOU?!
WHAM
WHAM

BUT THE ONLY OTHER MAGIC I'M ANY GOOD AT...
...IS MAKING IT RAIN...
NO ONE CAN DO THAT!!!
KERCRAKKK
HUH ...?!
UM, SORRY! WHAT DID YOU SAY?
DASH DASH
CRUMBLE
CRUMBLE
......

ALSO... WHY DID YOU MAKE A HOLE?
NOW LOOK HERE, YOU...
......
MUTTER
I KNEW IT... YOU'RE FROM THAT VILLAGE ...
HUH?
NEVER MIND. BRING ME A PEN AND PAPER...
TAK TAK TMP TMP
WILL THIS NOTEPAD FROM THE OTHER ROOM D—
SNATCH
EEP!
SCRITCH SCRITCH SCRITCH
......
HERE IS A MAP.
GIVE THIS LETTER TO THE CARPENTER...
WE HAVE TO GET HIM TO FIX THIS.
OH.
SURE.
NO RUSH OR ANYTHING.
SNAP
?!
IF YOU SAY SO...
TAK TAK

LEAVE IT TO ME ...!
STICK TO... NORMAL SPEEDS ...!
TAK
TAK
TAK

WELL...? WHAT DO YOU MAKE OF HIM?

...BACK AGAIN, MASTER ...?
JUST TAKING A PEEP. WON'T STAY LONG.

HE'S... SO SURE HE'S WEAK WHEN...
...HE'S ANY-THING BUT!

ONCE THE HEROES OF LEGEND SAVED THE WORLD...
...THEY LEFT IT BEHIND, SETTLING DOWN IN PEACE...
...IN A VILLAGE AT THE EDGE OF ALL MORTAL REALMS— KUNLUN.

FROM THERE, THEY PROTECT THE WORLD FROM CALAMITIES AND DEMON LORDS WITH NONE THE WISER.
AND LLOYD HAILS FROM THAT FABLED VILLAGE...!!

SUR-ROUNDED BY THE DESCEN-DANTS OF HEROES ...
...LLOYD GENUINELY IS THE WEAKEST KID IN TOWN.
HE ALSO LACKS SELF-CONFI-DENCE...
BUT LLOYD HAS A DREAM.

WORK HARD AND BECOME A SOLDIER, MY DEAR LLOYD.
DO IT FOR THE SAKE OF ACHIEVING YOUR OWN DREAM...
CAN SOMEONE REMIND ME WHAT COMMON SENSE IS AGAIN?
...AND ALSO MY HEART'S DESIRE ...!!
TAK
TAK
TAK
CAR-PENTER ...
CAR-PENTER ...
AND THUS, LLOYD'S LIFE IN THE CAPITAL HAS BEGUN.
OH? NO, WAIT...
THIS WAY?
UM...
THE HARSH (?) TEST TO BECOME A SOLDIER LIES AHEAD.

THIS IS THE STORY OF THIS BOY...
...AND THE PEOPLE AROUND HIM...

...WHO HAVE BEEN BOUND TOGETHER BY THE THREADS...
...OF VARIOUS MIS-UNDER-STAND-INGS.

...YOU KNOW HOW IT GOES.

—NOW, LET'S SEE... IN THE PARLANCE OF OUR TIMES, WE MIGHT CALL IT...

...THE TALE OF A KID FROM THE LAST DUNGEON BOONIES WHO MOVED TO A STARTER TOWN.
DOES THAT WORK?
OKAY! I'M GONNA GIVE IT EVERYTHING I'VE GOT!

THRILLED TO BE GETTING DELICIOUS, BALANCED MEALS

TAK
TAK
TAK
EAST SIDE, MARIE'S SHOP
TAK
TA
TA TAK
I'M BACK!
WANNABE SOLDIER BOY
LLOYD BELLADONNA
WELCOME BACK, LLOYD.
THANKS FOR TAKING CARE OF THE SHOPPING.
NO PROB-LEM!
I WAS A LITTLE NERVOUS AT FIRST, BUT...
COMMON SENSE IS ESSENTIAL FOR THE MILITARY ACADEMY ENTRANCE EXAM...
...TO PASS THE INTERVIEW AND SO ON.
SHOPPING'S A GOOD WAY TO GET USED TO LIFE IN THE BIG CITY!

YOU THOUGHT THAT FAR AHEAD FOR A COUNTRY BUMPKIN LIKE ME?
BOW
THANK YOU SO MUCH, MARIE!
WE'LL HAVE NONE OF THAT.
I DUNNO ABOUT COUN-TRY...

...BUT YOU'RE FROM KUNLUN...
LEGENDARY VILLAGE
KUNLUN
...WHERE THE DESCENDANTS OF HEROES DEFY SENSE... AND THE CONCEPT OF "NORMAL"!!

HE MAY BE STRONG, BUT IF HE FAILS THE INTERVIEW PORTION...
...SHE'LL BE A NIGHTMARE TO DEAL WITH...
MARIEEE...
...DO SOME-THIIING!
OH!
BY THE WAY, LLOYD...

I KNOW I SAID YOU COULD KEEP THE CHANGE...
...BUT DID YOU HAVE ENOUGH TO BEGIN WITH? PRICES ARE HIGH NOW, RIGHT?
THEY ARE?

YES, THAT'S RIGHT.
EARLIER, THE CARPENTER WAS TELLING ME ABOUT HOW—
!
GASP
MONSTERS ON THE CENTRAL ROAD?!
LAST CHAPTER'S HOLE (FIXED)
HE FIXED IT

AND A ROCKSLIDE ON THE ROAD OUT WEST!
NOTHING GETTING THROUGH EITHER WAY! THERE'RE NO CHEAP IMPORTS FROM FAR OFF TO BE HAD, AND PRICES ARE SKY-ROCKETING!

OUR LAST RAY OF HOPE'S THE JIOU EMPIRE, BUT DON'T THEY KNOW IT! THEY'RE MAKING US PAY THROUGH THE NOSE!
OUR COUNTRIES DON'T GET ALONG, AFTER ALL...
JIOU EMPIRE
MONSTER
MONEY
AZAMI KINGDOM
ANGRY MERCHANTS BLAMING THE EMPIRE FOR THE MONSTERS AND THE ROCKSLIDE HAVE SET TONGUES WAGGING.
THOSE MONSTERS HAVE EVEN BEGUN TO APPEAR IN TOWN.
THIS CAN ONLY FURTHER THE KING'S HOPES FOR WAR WITH JIOU...
BETTER KEEP THIS DANGEROUS TALK FROM LLOYD...
BUT IT SURE DOESN'T SOUND LIKE A COINCI-DENCE.

ROCKSLIDES, MONSTERS...
COULD THE JIOU EMPIRE REALLY BE BEHIND IT ALL...?
...?
IT WAS PLENTY!
GOT THE WOODEN PESTLE... MORTAR AND FLOUR...
...AND I HAD ENOUGH LEFT OVER TO BUY A PRESENT!
OH REALLY?
DIG DIG
HUH...?! OH, YOU SHOULDN'T HAVE... I'LL GIVE YOU MORE POCKET MONEY LATER.
HERE! A BROOCH FOR YOU!
TA-DAH
GLINT
EXPENSIVE TORTOISE-SHELL
EXPENSIVE METALWORK
SPARKLE
LUXURY ITEM
HOW MUCH DID YOU HAVE LEFT?!
THIS IS DEFINITELY WORTH MORE THAN THE AMOUNT I GAVE YOU THIS MORNING!!
WHERE AND HOW IN THE WORLD DID YOU EVEN GET THIS?!
EEEEEEEK!
WHERE? HOW...?
SPARKLE
SPARKLE

THERE WAS THIS RIVER ON THE WAY...
...AND THE WATER HAD DRIED UP. I MADE IT RAIN FOR THE PEOPLE COMPLAINING ABOUT MERCHANT SHIPS NOT BEING ABLE TO GET THROUGH!*
YOU'RE A LIFE-SAVER!
TAKE THIS IN RETURN!
MERCHANT
SPLOOOO-OOOSH
YOU RESTORED A DRIED-UP RIVER?!
※USING THE POWER OF ANCIENT RUNES
BUT THERE AREN'T ANY RIVERS EN ROUTE TO THE LOCAL SHOPS.
OH, I WAS AFTER SOME CHEAPER FLOUR...
DESTINATION
...SO I WENT TO A VILLAGE TWO MOUNTAINS OVER...*
IT WAS ON THE WAY BACK...
AZAMI KINGDOM
YOU WENT TO AN ENTIRELY DIFFER-ENT COUNTRY?!
※TRAVERSING MOUNTAINS TO SHOP IS NORMAL IN KUNLUN.
BUT WHEN ALL'S SAID AND DONE, I DID PAY FOR THE BROOCH!
WHILE ON THE WEST ROAD, I'D ALREADY SAVED A BUNCH ON THE FLOUR AND STUFF, SO I USED ALL THE MONEY I HAD ON ME...
THE WEST ROAD?
ISN'T THAT WHERE THE ROCKSLIDE THAT MIGHT SPARK A WAR IS ...?

YES! BOULDERS FROM A ROCKSLIDE HAD BLOCKED THE ROAD, YOU SEE!
SO I CLEANED THEM UP, AND THE MERCHANTS PRACTICALLY GAVE ME EVERYTHING AT NO COST!
THESE ARE IN THE WAY!
YOU'RE A GOD!
WE CAN GET THROUGH!!
HE SINGLE-HANDEDLY RESOLVED AN INFRA-STRUCTURE ISSUE AND AVERTED WAR !!!

IT WAS JUST A SIMPLE ERRAND TOO...
KUNLUN VILLAGERS REALLY ARE SOMETHING ELSE...
UM ...

I KNOW YOU'VE LEFT ME THE CLEANING AND ALL, BUT...
...I FELT LIKE I SHOULD RETURN THE FAVOR YOU'RE DOING ME BY LETTING ME STAY HERE FOR FREE...
!

AND SO I THOUGHT I COULD AT LEAST GET YOU A GIFT TO SAY THANKS.
PLEASE, TAKE IT.

......
I REALLY MUST...

...POUND SOME COMMON SENSE INTO HIM WITHOUT DELAY.
GOING TO ANOTHER COUNTRY JUST TO DO YOUR SHOPPING IS BAD ENOUGH, BUT...
...GUILE-LESSLY GIVING WOMEN PRESENTS LIKE THIS...

...IS JUST ASKING FOR TROUBLE.
LLOYD LEFT TO GO SHOPPING FOR A FEW HOURS AND SAVED THE REALM.
BUT TODAY'S MAIN STORY...

...IS ABOUT HOW LLOYD SAVED A GIRL WHILE OUT SHOPPING...
...AND CHANGED HER DESTINY FOREVER.
CASE 2
That Encounter Was Like a God Came in on a White Horse

RIGHT, LLOYD! ONE MORE ERRAND FOR YOU!
USE THIS MONEY TO BUY SOMETHING TO EAT!
PERSONAL FINANCE— NO, SOCIAL STUDIES, TAKE TWO!
THIS TIME, I'LL...
AND STAY IN AZAMI!!
AS LLOYD WAS PREPARING TO GO SHOPPING AGAIN...
...THE GIRL IN QUESTION...
...WAS WALKING THROUGH AZAMI'S SOUTH SIDE.
CLAMOR
SWAY...
BUSTLE
I NEED...

BUZZ
...TO BUY SOMETHING TO EAT AND HEAD BACK SOON...
CHATTER
CHATTER
HFF...
HFF...
BUZZ
SWAY
SWAY
HEY! HEY!
I HEAR IT'S ALMOST TIME FOR AZAMI'S FOUNDATION DAY FESTIVAL!
LET'S TAKE IN ALL THE SIGHTS WE CAN BEFO—
WAH!
BUMP
GOOD IDEA!

WHAT'S WITH HER?
A HOOD ON A SUNNY DAY LIKE THIS? CREEPY.
......
LOTS OF PEOPLE AT THIS HOUR...
HUSTLE
I SHOULD HAVE WAITED FOR NIGHT.
BUSTLE
???
SELEN HEMEIN
GRRROWL
BUT I CAN'T BEAR THESE HUNGER PAINS...
!
YOU GETTING HUNGRY, GIRLIE?
HUH?!
BUY SOME OF MY WARES!

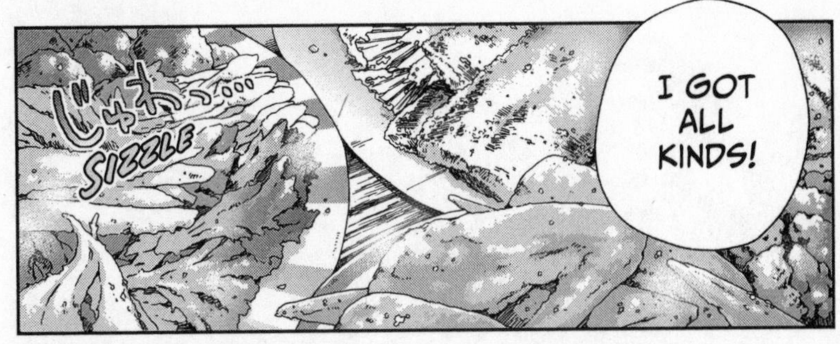
I GOT ALL KINDS!
じゅわっ
SIZZLE

GULP
UM...
THIS COSTS MONEY?
?
UM...
I DO HAVE MY PURSE, BUT...
WHAT'S WRONG?
I'VE...
SORRY, HOW DO I...?
BUSTLE
HUSTLE
I'VE NEVER BEEN SHOPPING.
I DON'T KNOW HOW IT WORKS...
HAAAH...
!
GIRLIE... BEHIND YOU!

EXCUSE ME.
MAY WE SEE SOME IDENTIFI-CATION?
THIS MAY SOUND RUDE...
...BUT WITH THE FOUNDA-TION DAY FESTIVAL NEAR...
...WE'VE INCREASED PATROLS.
THERE ARE RUMORS THAT SOMEONE'S RELEASING MONSTERS ONTO THE STREETS TOO.

AND YOU THINK ...
...I'M SUSPICIOUS?
AREN'T YOU? DRESSED LIKE THAT...

IF YOU'VE GOT NOTHING TO HIDE...
...TAKE OFF THAT HOOD!
WHOOSH
!

SLAP

!!
Y-YOUR HEAD...

THE BELT PRIN-CESS ...?!!
THE FAMOUS LOCAL LORD'S DAUGH-TER?!
WANNABE SOLDIER
SELEN HEMEIN
AKA. THE BELT PRINCESS
THE RUMORS SHE WAS RECRUITED WERE TRUE...
MURMUR
THE BELT PRINCESS ...?
MURMUR
I'VE NEVER SEEN ANYTHING LIKE HER...
WE'RE DRAWING A CROWD.

THAT'S WHAT I WAS TRYING TO AVOID!
DASH
AH...!
WHO'S THAT GIRL?
MURMUR
A NOBLE-WOMAN FROM THE CENTRAL REGION.
MURMUR
SELEN HEMEIN.
THE CURSED BELT PRINCESS.
THIS BELT...

ONE OF MANY RARE ARTIFACTS...
...WAS IN MY FATHER'S COLLEC-TION.
!
WAAAAH...!

MILADY SELEN?!
AH ...!
THE CURSED BELT.
NOTHING COULD REMOVE IT. ACADEMICS AND MONKS ALIKE ABANDONED THEIR ATTEMPTS TO DO SO.
AT FIRST, PEOPLE FELT PITY...
...THEN, THEY BEGAN TO LOATHE THE VERY SIGHT OF ME.

I FLED, SPENDING ALL MY TIME IN MY ROOM.

THEN, ONE DAY...

ONLY THE POWER OF SOMEONE TRULY STRONG CAN FREE YOU FROM THAT BELT.

THAT IS ALL I CAN TELL YOU.
BUT...
...IF YOU SEARCH AND FIND NONE WHO CAN BREAK THE BELT'S CURSE...

...YOU YOURSELF...
...MUST OBTAIN THE POWER TO DEFEAT IT.

THOSE WORDS WERE MY ONLY HOPE.
WSH

I TRAINED...
...DAY AFTER DAY...
...ALONE IN MY ROOM, CARING NOTHING FOR MY APPEARANCE...
BEFORE I KNEW IT, THE WORLD HAD DUBBED ME...
..."THE CURSED BELT PRINCESS."
THE CURSE REMAINS.
BUT WORD OF MY STRENGTH REACHED THE CAPITAL...
...AND I WAS RECRUITED TO ENLIST.
TAK TAK
IT'S ALWAYS LIKE THIS.

I DID NOTHING WRONG BUT WAS ACCOSTED.
HAAH...
I OUGHT TO HAVE COME WHEN THE CROWDS THINNED.
STAGGER...
THAT MAD DASH USED UP THE LAST OF MY STRENGTH...
GROWWWL

I HAVE TO EAT SOMETHING.
I HAVE RICE, BUT I'VE NEVER COOKED...
RECENT MEALS
DRY RICE
EATEN STRAIGHT (ALL SHE CAN DO)
IF THEY'D JUST LET ME BUY SOMETHING BACK THERE...

THAT FRIED FOOD LOOKED SOOOO GOOD...
IT IS!
WAFT
WAFT
OH YES! IT SMELLED JUST LIKE THIS...
SNIFF
SNIFF
OH! KEBABS!

WHIP
OH... DEEP-FRIED ...!!
FRESH OFF THE GRILL?
BUT HOW DO I BUY THEM?
THAT, THEY ARE!
I'LL TAKE ONE.
NO, TWO!
I SEE! YOU HAND OVER MONEY, AND THEY GIVE YOU THINGS!
I CAN DO THAT.
TAKE OUT MONEY.
HAND IT OVER.
GET FOOD.
TAKE OUT...
HAND OVER...!
GET FOOD...
GOT IT!
WAIT UNTIL THERE'S NO ONE NEAR THE SHOP!
IF I HIDE HERE, NO ONE WILL SEE ME.
STAY OUT OF TROUBLE.

WANT ONE?
JUMP
...... HUH ...?!
SORRY IF I STARTLED YOU.
YOU WERE WATCHING ME BUY THESE, RIGHT?
I THOUGHT YOU MIGHT BE HUNGRY.

YOU SAW ME?!
BUT I WAS BEING STEALTHY!
I'M GOOD AT IT TOO, YOU KNOW?!
HUH? YOU WERE?

HA HA, GOOD ONE!
NO NEED FOR THAT!
YOU'RE NOT A WOOD-CUTTER!
WOODCUTTING FUNDAMENTAL (IN KUNLUN)
HIDE YOURSELF, SNEAK UP, ONE SHOT!
WHOEVER HEARD OF A STEALTHY WOOD-CUTTER?
?

THIS KID SEEMS WEIRD...
WHO IS HE?
OH!
SHOULD I NOT HAVE BOUGHT THIS FOR YOU?

IN THAT CASE, SORR—
GROWL

......
GURGLE GRRR...

SMILE
GRR...
YOUR FIRST TIME SHOPPING, HUH?
I GET THAT! I WAS REALLY NERVOUS MY FIRST TIME TOO.
DIDN'T WANT TO BE RUDE...
WHERE I'M FROM, WE USUALLY TRADE ONE ITEM FOR ANOTHER.

BUT IN THE CITY, YOU CAN JUST RELAX...
...AND ACT NATU-RAL!
......

I'M NOT SO GOOD AT THAT...
DON'T WORRY! CITY FOLK ARE USED TO IT!

THEY'RE NOTHING LIKE THE DWARF VILLAGE CRAFTSMEN ...
...WHO'LL COME AFTER YOU WITH AN AXE AT THE SLIGHTEST OFFENSE!
THE KUNLUN VILLAGE
DAILY LIFE
UGH.
HUH?!
DWARF...?!

......
......
OH,
YOU'VE NEVER MET ONE? THEY'RE REALLY SHORT.
Dwarf
UH...
I'VE NEVER MET A DWARF, BUT...
...I'VE SEEN THE NAME.
OH, I SEE!

FAIRY TALE
HE'S JOKING, RIGHT?
...IN FAIRY TALES ANYWAY.
ARE DWARVES FAMOUS?
UHHHH...

...SOUNDS LIKE AN URBAN LEGEND TO SELEN.
COMMON SENSE IN KUNLUN...
GLANCE
LLOYD WAS NOT JOKING! THIS HAD ACTUALLY HAPPENED TO HIM.
?
?
?!

IF YOU EVER MEET A DWARF...
MAKE SURE YOU MEET THEIR EYE.
WHY WOULD HE SPIN THESE TALL TALES?
FIRST, THE WOODCUTTER THING, NOW THIS...

OH!

HE'S BEING SILLY...
...TO PUT ME AT EASE.
WITH ELVES, TRY NOT TO HAVE IRON ON YOU.
HE'S NICE.
THESE ARE TRUE FACTS!
THANKS FOR YOUR HELP. MAY I REPAY YOU?
MONEY?
OH NO! DON'T WORRY ABOUT IT!

SOUNDS LIKE I JUST STOLE YOUR CHANCE TO PRACTICE SHOPPING, AFTER ALL!
OH, I KNOW!

WHY NOT TAKE THAT MONEY AND BUY YOURSELF A SECOND KEBAB?
HUH?!

UH, I WASN'T TRYING TO PRAC-TICE...
DON'T WORRY, I'LL BE RIGHT BEHIND YOU.
AH...

JUST BE CON-FIDENT!
CLENCH
......
HE'S WATCHING OVER ME.
TKK
IT'S BEEN A LONG TIME...
...SINCE I HAD ANYTHING LIKE A NORMAL CONVERSATION.

VOOOM

!!
THOSE SOLDIERS!
GASP
IF THEY SEE ME, IT'LL BE TROUBLE ...

SPIN
OH NO!

IF THEY CATCH ME...
...WITH HIM WATCHING ...?
!

HE'LL SEE...
...MY FACE!!

EVERYONE WHO DOES FLINCHES IN HORROR...
...THANKS TO THIS HIDEOUS BELT...

IF HE KNOWS HOW HIDEOUS I AM...
...I'M SURE HE'LL ......

AH! THERE SHE IS!
!!

WHAT'S WRONG? YOU'RE ALMOST AT THE STALL!
ONE MORE STEP!
WHOOSH
YOU CAN DO...
...IT —?

HFF!
HFF!
TAK
TAK
TAK
HFFFF!
HAAH...
I THINK I GOT AWAY CLEAN.
TAK...
BUT...
CRUNCH

...WHERE AM I?

THIS PLACE IS FILTHY.
I MIGHT BE ON THE EAST SIDE...

I'M LOST, AREN'T I?
HOW DO I GET BACK TO THE INN...?
WAFT...
?!
THAT STENCH...

IT'S VILE!
MUST BE SOME ROTTING TRASH.
UGH, I SHOULD NEVER HAVE COME HERE...
......
BUT THIS IS BETTER THAN HIM SEEING MY FACE.
I JUST GOTTA FIND MY WAY OUT.
SLIDE
TMP
TMP
TMP
SPLAT
!
OH, THAT'S WHERE THE...
...GAR-BAGE SM...

SQUELCH
AN... ANIMAL?
A DEAD ONE ...?!
!

LOOK AT THE STATE OF IT!
IT'S LIKE SOMETHING...
GRIND
RUSTLE
...WAS EATING IT...!
KRRK
THUD

CLICK

SKREEE...
EEEEE...
SNAP
KRIK KRIK
A BUG ...?!!
NO, THAT'S...
CLICK
CLICK
CRACK
SQUIRT
SQUIRT
THE RUMORS ...

THERE ARE RUMORS...
...THAT SOMEONE'S RELEASING **MONSTERS** ONTO THE STREETS...
!
SKREEEE
GRIND
GRIND
GRIND
CRACK
QUIVER
QUIVER
IT SAW ME!
SHHNG
MY SWORD!

KERWHAM
CRUMBLE
CRUMBLE
CRUMBLE
UNH ...!
THUD
THUD
SKIIID
WHAP
WHOOOM
CRAP.....!

TAP
...HUH?!
HUP!

HEAVE!
HO!
CRACK
?!!

HUH ...?!
NO WAY...
WOW.
SO MANY BUGS IN THE CITY!
GRAB

TOSS
YOU OKAY?
WHAAAAT?
WOBBLE
KATHUNK
WOBBLE

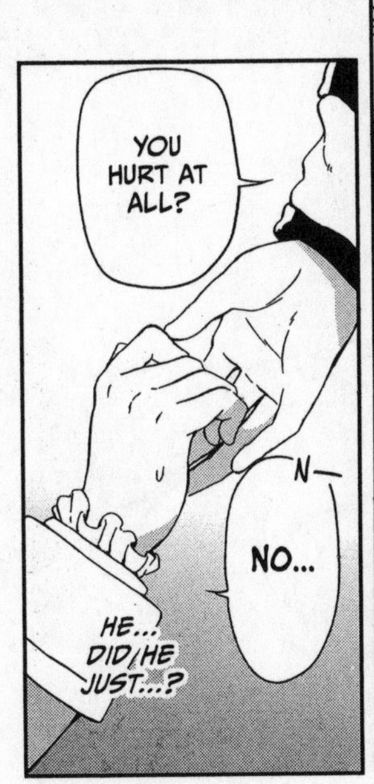
YOU HURT AT ALL?
N—
NO...
HE... DID HE JUST...?

?
HE JUST BEAT A MONSTER!
HE'S NOT A WARRIOR OR A SOLDIER OR ANY-THING!!
LIKE IT WAS NOTHING ...!

DID YOU PANIC AS YOU GOT NEAR THE STALL?
I SAW YOU RUN OFF.
DON'T WORRY.
PAT
WHEW...
PAT
WELL, AT LEAST HE DIDN'T SEE MY FACE.
EVEN IF HE HAS THE WRONG IDEA...

OH!
LOOK AT YOUR FACE.
FWIP

SPIN!!
......!!

I LET DOWN MY GUARD!
HE SAW MY FACE!!
......

NOW, HE TOO...
...WILL THINK I'M CREEPY.
UM...

LET ME JUST...
...GET THE DIRT OFF YOUR FACE.

THERE! ALL CLEAN NOW.
GASP
YANK
OH NO!

I NEED TO GET HOME AND START DINNER!
......
GLANCE

WELL ...
UM ...!
!

WHAT?
?
CLENCH
I...

WHAP!!
MY...
MY NAME'S SELEN!

OH, WHERE ARE MY MANNERS?
I'M LLOYD.
BEAM!!

BYYYE!
KICK
HUH ?!

TAK
TAK
TAK
TAK
TAK
WHIRL
TWIRL
TAK
THNK
SEE YOU AROUND!

AND LIKE THAT, LLOYD WAS GONE.
SELEN WATCHED HIM GO...

...GAZING AFTER HIM A WHILE...
...TRYING TO PRESERVE THE FEEL OF HIS HAND ON HER CHEEK.
BLUSHHH

TAK TAK TAK TAK
HMM... THAT BELT...
SOME SORT OF BIG CITY FASHION TREND ...?
BOING
BOING

♪
♪
♪
TAK
TAK
TAK
TAK

TEE-HEE...
TWIRL

I GOT EXCITED AND BOUGHT WAY TOO MUCH!

WILL I SEE HIM AGAIN?
I HOPE I DO.

IF I STAY IN THE CITY, I'M SURE I WILL.
TEE-HEE...
!
CHATTER
CHATTER

GEH.
THE RUMORS WERE TRUE?

THE BELT PRINCESS REALLY DOES WANNA ENLIST.
HE BEARS THE MARK OF A LOCAL LORD...
THE LIDO-CAINE FAMILY...
WANNABE SOLDIER
ALLAN TOIN LIDOCAINE

THEY'RE HEAVILY DECO-RATED.
SEEMS FORMI-DABLE... BEST TO AVOID...
HEY!
STRIDE
STRIDE

DO YOU HAVE ANY IDEA...
...HOW MUCH YOU'VE DAMAGED OUR REPU-TATION?
!

THAT THING ON YOUR FACE...
...HAS RUMORS FLYING!
"ALL THE LOCAL LORDS ARE WEIRDOS," THEY SAY!

I'M SICK...
...OF HEARING ABOUT IT.

STRIDE
STRIDE
DON'T YOU DARE IGNORE ME!
GRRR...
DAMN.
WHAT A FREAK.
TURN
WEL-COME BA—
EEP!
TAK
TAK
TAK
TAK
TAK

RIGHT.

MY CLOTHES ARE FILTHY!

I NEED TO WASH THEM!

I MIGHT SEE HIM AGAIN, AFTER ALL.

FWSH
EVEN WITH THIS FACE ...
...IT'S BETTER IF I'M CLEAN.

SPLASH

SPLISH
SPLASH
SPLOSH
LLOYD.

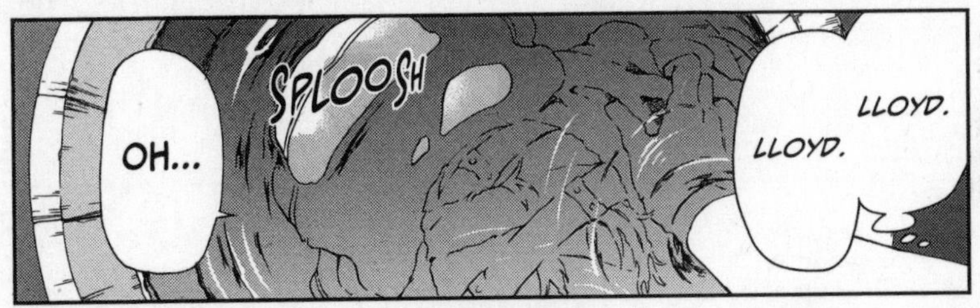
LLOYD.
LLOYD.
SPLOOSH
OH...

I SHOULD TRY SOME MAKEUP!
JUST...
...IN CASE WE MEET AGAIN...
IF I MAKE MYSELF PRETTY
......

PRETTY ......!
DRIP...
HOW CAN I?! WITH THIS THING ON ME ...?!
I IMAGINED MYSELF IN MAKEUP WITH NO HOOD...
...MEETING HIM AGAIN...
I JUST WANT TO SHOW HIM...
...A SLIGHTLY PRETTIER VERSION OF ME...

IS THAT TOO MUCH TO ASK?
SNIFF
IF ONLY...
...IT WEREN'T FOR THIS BELT...!!!
GLINT
GRAB
I WANT IT OFF...
...EVEN IF IT TAKES MY FACE WITH IT!
WHOOSH

UNFURL
HUH ...?
NO WAY...
IT CAME OFF...? BUT HOW ...?!
UNFURL
—THE POWER OF SOMEONE TRULY STRONG...

ONLY THE POWER OF SOMEONE TRULY STRONG CAN FREE YOU FROM THAT BELT.
...SOMEONE TRULY STRONG...
OH...
IT WAS HIM...
HE DID THIS.
FATE BROUGHT US TOGETHER.
HAVING SAVED A GIRL WITHOUT REALIZING, LLOYD...
AUGH, LLOYD!

MM?
YOU'RE USING THAT RUNE TO CLEAN AGAIN?!
WIPING THE TABLE...
OH!

WELL, IT MAKES EVERYTHING SPOTLESS!
WISDOM OF THE ANCIENTS—
SEN-CHANT RUNE
NOT JUST THIS RAG EITHER!
I USE IT ON MY HANDKERCHIEF...
LISTEN UP, KID!
IT'S SO HANDY!
AUUUGH!
I CAAAN'T!
THE CURSE ...
...WAS BROKEN BY THE DISENCHANT RUNE.
BUT EVEN A CHANCE ENCOUNTER...
...CAN FEEL LIKE THE WHEEL OF DESTINY TURNING.

AND SO TIME PASSED...
CREAK
GOOD LUCK, LLOYD!
OH...
THANK YOU!
...AND THE BIG DAY ARRIVED.

AT LONG LAST, THE AZAMI MILITARY ACADEMY GENERAL ADMISSIONS EXAM...
...IS ABOUT TO GET UNDER-WAY!
WOOSH

IF YOU INSIST...

NOT EVERY JOKE FROM THE NOVELS MADE IT IN!

Suppose
a Kid from the
LAST DUNGEON
BOONIES Moved
to a
Starter Town

OH HOH! I SEE...
OHHH, NOT BAD—
WOW, YOU GOT HER?!
YOU REALLY OUTDID YOURSELF THIS YEAR.
AN UNPRECEDENTED SELECTION!
RIGHT, MERTHO-PHAN?
THESE ALL YOUR DOING?
......

ALL FOR THE PEACE OF THE REALM.
SKILL MUST OUTWEIGH STATUS...
...OR WE'LL GET NOWHERE.
AZAMI MILITARY COLONEL AND MILITARY ACADEMY INSTRUCTOR MERTHOPHAN DEXTRO
YOU AGREE, CHOLINE?
SURE.
I KINDA DO?
AZAMI MILITARY ACADEMY INSTRUCTOR CHOLINE STERASE

BUT EVEN FOR PEACE, THAT ONE'S A BIT MUCH!
THAT MERCENARY IS A LEGIT VILLAIN! THERE'S A WARRANT OUT FOR HER ARREST!
WE MADE A DEAL. NOT AN ISSUE.
IF SHE ENLISTS, THE WARRANT IS RE-SCINDED.

WELL, WELL...
PULLING STRINGS FOR...
OH?

WHERE ARE YOU GOING?
PREPPIN' FOR THE TEST!
I'M IN CHARGE OF THE WRITTEN MAGIC STUFF!

SEE YA LATER!
PUT THIS BACK FOR ME?
HAAH...
THE BELT PRINCESS CAME TOO.
SHOULD BE A STRONG LINEUP.

WITH THEIR STRENGTH, THE REALM'S FUTURE IS—
HRM?!
BWFF!
WH—
WHO'S THAT BOY?!

THERE MUST BE SOME-WHERE I CAN SIT DOWN...

RUMMMBLE

HE LOOKS INCREDIBLY FEARSOME ?!!

CASE 3
This Stroke of Luck Was Like Finding a Wish-Granting Magic Flower Growing in Your Backyard

THE CENTRAL SQUARE BELOW AZAMI CASTLE...
...IS A POPULAR TOURIST ATTRACTION FEATURING A BRONZE STATUE OF THE KING HIMSELF.

THE STATUE IS IN NOTICEABLY BETTER SHAPE THAN AND FAR MORE HANDSOME THAN THE REAL THING.
A TRIBUTE TO THE KING'S VANITY...
THE REAL KING'S A FAT OLD MAN.
SO THE LOCALS HOLD IT IN CON-TEMPT.
APPLI-CANTS FOR THE ACAD-EMY...
...ARE MILLING AROUND THE STATUE.
SKRIT
SKRIT
I CAN USE A LOT OF THESE PEOPLE.

SMELLS LIKE MONEY!
WANNABE SOLDIER THE ONE-ARMED MERCENARY RIHO FLAVIN
THIS "VILLAIN" IS NOT ABOUT TO MISS A THING.

INFAMOUS FOR TURNING ON EMPLOYERS SHE DISLIKES, WANTED FOR ASSAULT AND BORDER VIOLATIONS...
...SHE HAS A REP FOR BEING A FOR-MIDABLE MERCE-NARY.
THE SECRET TO HER SUCCESS IS BEING ABLE TO TELL APART THE MANAGEABLE EMPLOYERS, THE EASYGOING TEAMMATES...

WILL THEY BRING IN MONEY? WILL THEY MAKE POWERFUL PAWNS?
EVEN NOW, SHE'S IN THE PROCESS OF ANALYZING THE WORTH OF THE PEOPLE AROUND HER.
ARE YOU THE BELT PRINCESS ...?!
STIR...
!

THE CURSED BELT PRINCESS HERSELF?
SHE LOOKS DIFFERENT FROM THE STORIES...
IS THAT THE BELT ON HER WAIST?
SHE BROKE THE CURSE?
FORMER CURSED BELT PRINCESS SELEN HEMEIN
SO THE BELT DOES COME OFF?
WHY DIDN'T YOU DO THAT SOONER?!
ALLAN TOIN LIDOCAINE.
ALLAN.
LIDOCAINE? ANOTHER HEIR TO A LOCAL LORD...
LOOKS GOOD WITH AN AXE, BUT... TOURNAMENT-STYLE... USELESS IN WAR.
SCRITCH SCRIT
THE BELT PRINCESS HAS TRAINED HARD BUT HAS NO COMBAT EXPERIENCE...
HAVE TO CHOOSE CAREFULLY FOR TEAM JOBS, BUT RICH PEOPLE CAN BE USEFUL ON THE RIGHT ONES.
NOW, THEN.
TIME TO FACE REALITY...
SHUT

RUMBLE
WHO'S THIS BEAST?!!
WHEW.
FINALLY FOUND A PLACE TO SIT!

PROBABLY THE LAST OPEN SPOT...
GLANCE GLANCE
HE LOOKS ORDINARY, BUT HE TOTALLY ISN'T!
ONE WRONG MOVE, AND MY LIFE IS FORFEIT!

NEVER FIGURED THERE'D BE CANDIDATES LIKE THIS! I WANNA RUN FOR IT SO BAD!
UM, CAN I ASK YOU SOMETHING?
LOOM
JOLT
YEEK!

IS THAT...
...A MECHANICAL ARM?

CRAP! I RAISED IT ON REFLEX!

HE MIGHT TAKE THAT AS A SIGN OF AGGRESSION!
SHWP
BETTER PICK MY NEXT WORDS WITH CARE! MY FATE'S ON THE LINE!!

A
ADMIT IT.
OH YES! IT'S A MECHANICAL ARM.
THEN IT FEELS NO PAIN!
RIP
RIP
RIP
RIP
AUGHHHHH!!
NOPE, HE'LL JUST KILL ME!

B
LIE.
I WAS BORN THIS WAY.
LIAR!
RIP
RIP
RIP
AUGHHHHH!!
NOPE, HE'LL KILL ME THERE TOO!! THAT LEAVES...?

STAY MUM.
SAY SOME-THING!
NO WAY OUT!!
MY LIFE...IS OVER...
RIP
RIP
RIP
AUGHHHHHHH!
SOB

UM, I'M SORRY! I DIDN'T MEAN TO PRY.
I JUST THOUGHT IT LOOKED REALLY COOL!
COULDN'T HELP MYSELF...
EVEN THE DEVIL SMILES!
HA HA...
I JUST GOT HERE FROM THE BOONIES, SO I DON'T KNOW ANYONE!
MY NAME'S LLOYD BELLA-DONNA.
IF I DON'T TAKE HIS HAND, DEATH AWAITS!
SHP
UH... RIHO FLAVIN.
N-NICE TO MEET YOU...
......

TREMBLE TREMBLE TREMBLE TREMBLE
OHHH, LLOYD LLOYD LLOYD LLOYD LLOYD LLOYD LLOYD LLOYD LLOYD LLOYD LLOYD LLOYD LLOYD.
LLOYD LLOYD LLOYD LLOYD LLOYD LLOYD
HFF!
HFF!
THE BELT PRINCESS?! WHAT'S WRONG WITH HER?!
TREMBLE
TREMBLE
I HAVE ENOUGH PROBLEMS ALREADY!
OH!

SELEN, RIGHT?!
YOU'RE APPLYING TOO?
YES!
I'M SELEN HEMEIN, AND I'M ALL YOURS!!
THE KEBAB GIRL!
Y-YOU ARE?
I FOUND YOU AT LAST! THE DAYS WITHOUT YOU WERE NOTHING BUT AGONY!
THEY KNOW EACH OTHER ...?
MY CHANCE TO SCRAM!
SNEAK
SNEAK

AND...
...WHO MIGHT YOU BE?
CLAMP
DAMN YOU FOR FOILING MY ES-CAPE!!
LET ME FLEE!
?
IT SEEMS LIKE YOU AND LLOYD WERE GETTING COZY?!
DOOM
DOOM
COZY?! ARE YOU BLIND?!
CAN THOSE EYES SEE?

THIS IS RIHO!
WE JUST MET.
OH MY!
YOU DID? I THOUGHT SHE WAS A ROMANTIC RIVAL!
RO-MANTIC, SHMANTIC! I'M PEEING MYSELF HERE!

WHAT A WEIRD PAIRING.
THE DAUGHTER OF A LOCAL LORD AND A COUNTRY BUMPKIN...

I'VE GOT IT!!
THEY'RE FROM DIFFERENT WALKS OF LIFE, BUT JUST LOOK AT HOW CLOSE THEY SEEM...
I DIDN'T THINK I'D SEE YOU AGAIN!
OUR MEETING AGAIN LIKE THIS... IT MUST BE FATE!
THESE TWO MUST HAVE HISTORY!
LLOYD MAY HAVE TERRIFYING POWER...
...BUT IF I WORK HIS CONNECTION WITH THE BELT PRINCESS...
GO!
JOB

...I CAN PROFIT!
MONEY
MONEY
...I CAN PULL OFF ANY JOB, BIG OR SMALL!!
WITH THEM UNDER MY THUMB, FORGET PETTY ARMY MISSIONS...
RINGMASTER
GO GET 'EM, SIR LLOYD!!
WILL DO!
BIG SCORE
ACTUALLY, THEY'RE PERFECT STRANGERS.

HEH!
ALL RIGHTY THEN...

BWAM
BWAM
THIS COULD BE LUCRATIVE!!
BWAM
MY SHOT AT THE BIG TIME!
BWAM
WOW! I MADE FRIENDS!
BWAM
BUT FIRST, I'VE GOTTA PASS THIS TEST!
SMAK SMAK
BWAM
BWAM
BWAM
BWAM
LLOYD! LLOYD! LLOYD! LLOYD!
LLOYD! LLOYD! LLOYD! LLOYD!
BWAM
THINGS ARE GETTING WEIRD OVER THERE...
HEH! HEH! HEH! HEH! HEH!
HEE HEE HEE!
HEE HEE HEE HEE
TEE-HEE! HEE HEE HEE HEE!
?

ALL RIGHT! APPLICANTS, FALL INTO GROUPS AS LISTED!
LET'S GET THIS COMBAT TEST UNDER-WAY!!

THUD
SELECT YOUR WEAPON AND ATTACK THE DUMMY WITH IT!
YOU CAN USE YOUR OWN WEAPON IF YOU LIKE.
MURMUR
IRON PLATES ...
SO MANY LAYERS...
MURMUR
WE'LL BE LOOKING AT AGILITY AND COMFORT WITH THE WEAPON.
WHEN WE CALL YOUR NAME, ANSWER AND STEP FORWARD!

GROUP TWO, OVER HERE!
THOSE TWO ARE IN THE OTHER GROUP, HUH?
!

MUTTER
OH, THAT'S ...
WELL WORTH THE EFFORT TO GATHER THEM HERE...
WITH THEM FIGHTING FOR THEIR COUNTRY, WE'LL BE READY FOR ANY THREAT.
MUTTER

YO, MERTHO-PHAN!
THE ONE-ARMED ...
NOT GOING TO DROP OUT NOW, ARE YOU?

HEH, DON'T MAKE ME LAUGH.
CAN'T PASS UP THAT DEAL TO FLUSH MY SINS AWAY.
YOU SURE WENT ALL-OUT FOR THIS RECRUIT-MENT BUSINESS, THOUGH.

ALL FOR THE FUTURE OF THE REALM.
RELATIONS WORSENING WITH OUR NEIGHBORS... THE PRINCESS MISSING... OUR STABILITY DEPENDS ON A STRONG MILITARY.
HEH HEH...
SO THAT BRINGS ME TO MY QUES-TION...

RUMBLE RUMBLE RUMBLE RUMBLE
WHO THE HELL IS THAT KID?!
NO CLUE.
RUMBLE RUMBLE
YOU DIDN'T SCOUT HIM?!

D'YOU KNOW HOW DANGER-OUS HE IS?!
I'M AS SHOCKED AS YOU ARE!
I REALLY HAVE NO IDEA!
I CAN'T SEE.
MYSELF INCLU-DED...
...HE COULD TAKE ON EVERYONE HERE AT ONCE AND WIN!

I WAS WORRIED MY INSTINCTS WERE GOING HAYWIRE.
AT A GLANCE, HE'S JUST ANOTHER COUNTRY BRAT...
...WHICH IS EVEN SCARIER.

EITHER WAY, HE'S HERE TO ENLIST.
WITH HIM ON OUR SIDE, OUR ARMY WILL BE UNMATCHED FOR DECADES.

EVEN IF WAR BROKE OUT TOMORROW, WE'D BE SURE TO WIN.
I'M CERTAIN HE'S A GIFT FROM THE GODS.
GODS, HUH?

I KNOW YOU'RE CURIOUS...
...BUT I MUST REMAIN IMPARTIAL DURING TESTING.
BACK IN LINE! GET DISQUALIFIED, AND YOU'RE A CRIMINAL AGAIN.
YEAH, YEAH.

YOU SEEM CONFIDENT.
SURE YOU CAN PASS?

KRAAANG
THUD
YEAH.
THAT'S WHY YOU SCOUTED ME, COLONEL.

HOW...?! THAT WAS WELDED ON!
EASY.
MY PARTNER'S MADE OF MITHRIL.
HANDY, FOR SURE... BUT TERRIBLY HIGH MAINTE-NANCE.
SO HELP A GIRL OUT, WOULD YA?
YEP ...
THAT'S WHY I NEED LLOYD AND SELEN...
...TO PASS THIS THING TOO...
...SO I CAN RAKE IT IN OFF 'EM!!
CLANG
YAH! YAH! YAH! YAH!
AIYAH!!
CLANG
CLANG
CLANG

THAT'S ENOUGH!
SHING
ALLAN TOIN LIDO-CAINE...
WOW...
COULD YOU WIELD THAT AXE?
COULDN'T EVEN LIFT IT!

HE COMES FROM A DECORATED LINEAGE.
HE AGREED TO ENLIST ON THE CONDITION WE MAKE HIM AN OFFICER FORTHWITH.
A VERY AMBITIOUS MAN...

AMBITION MEANS A STRONG WILL.
HE DOESN'T RELY ON HIS NOBLE BIRTH... HE WILL BE AN ASSET.
FWIP
NEXT! LLOYD BELLA-DONNA!

OH!
FFERE!
CHOMP
OW!
HE BIT HIS TONGUE ?!

HEH HEH!
HERKY
HA!
JERKY
HE LOOKS POSI-TIVELY WEAK...

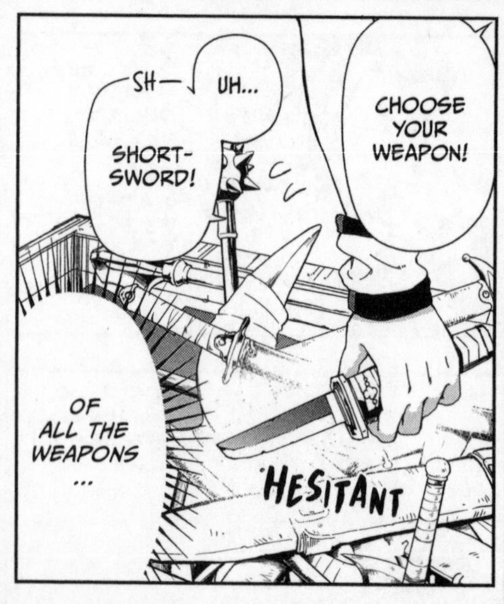
CHOOSE YOUR WEAPON!
UH...
SH—
SHORT-SWORD!
HESITANT
OF ALL THE WEAPONS ...

NO, IF HE'S FOCUSED ON SPEED...
MERTHOPHAN!

THEY'RE CALLING FOR YOU!
ACK!
MUST IT BE NOW?
WANTS TO WATCH
THAT'S VERY OUT OF CHARAC-TER FOR YOU!

RIGHT, CAN'T CONCERN MYSELF WITH ANY ONE INDI-VIDUAL.
THAT BOY WILL PASS THIS TEST.
I'LL OBSERVE HIS POWER ONCE HE'S ENLISTED.
HOW-EVER...

...LITTLE DID MERTHOPHAN KNOW...
RIGHT, TAKE A SWING AT THE DUMMY!
DOESN'T MATTER IF YOU CUT IT IN HALF!
BWAH HA HA!
HEH HEH!
IN HALF ...?!

IT LOOKS SO EASY TO CUT IN HALF...
MAYBE THERE'S SOME TRICK TO IT... WHAT COULD I BE MISSING ...?
NO WAY HE CAN!
HE'S TINY!
...THIS BOY'S **COMMON SENSE** WAS AS OUTLANDISH AS HIS STRENGTH.

THE LAST GUY DIDN'T EVEN SCRATCH IT...
NORMALLY, YOU'D EASILY DESTROY IRON DOING THAT!
STARE
I FEEL LIKE SOME-ONE'S OVERES-TIMATING ME...
TREMBLE
I GET IT NOW!
HE DOESN'T.
THIS TEST IS ABOUT SWINGS AND POSTURE ...
...WHICH MEANS...
COME ON.

...I'M NOT SUPPOSED TO DEFEAT THE DUMMY...
I'M SUPPOSED TO DO A QUICK, RHYTHMICAL COMBO!
POSTURE 10 SWINGS 9 ARTISTRY 10
YOU PASS!
WOW!
GOT IT!
HE DON'T GOT IT.
PLONK
LLOYD BELLA-DONNA! HURRY UP!!
QUIT THINKING!
R-RIGHT!
DASH
NICE AND EASY...
EASY DOES IT...

TIPTOE
TIPTOE
DON'T BREAK IT.
KEEP...

...IT RHYTHMICAL...
TIPTOE
C'MON!
HEH HEH!

COMBO!!
SNIKT
TAK

CRUMBLE
CRUMBLE
CRUMBLE
HOOOOW?!!
CRASHHH

YOU PULLIN' MY LEG?! HEY!
WHAT HAP-PENED?!
OH NOOOO! NOW I'VE DONE IIIIIIT...
NOW WHAT? THEY CAN'T BELIEVE I SCREWED UP SO BAD!
SIR, WHAT WAS THAT?!
TOO FAST FOR THEM TO SEE ↑

HMM...
IT WAS LIKE THE DUMMY COLLAPSED BEFORE HE TOUCHED IT...
DID HE MOVE TOO FAST FOR THE EYE TO SEE?
←DIDN'T SEE IT EITHER

NAH, NOT A KID LIKE THAT.
IT MUST HAVE BEEN WEAKENED BY ALLAN'S ATTACKS!
THAT'S WHAT YOU GET FOR DITH-ERING!
NEXT!!
UUUUUGH...
←DIDN'T SEE OR HEAR

UGH...
D-DON'T GIVE UP YET!

BLAZE
BLAZE
THE WRITTEN TEST AND INTERVIEW ARE STILL TO COME!!
LLOYD... I CAN'T WAIT TO SEE YOUR INCREDIBLE RESULTS!
UH...
LLOYD BELLA-DONNA'S COMBAT SCORE IS A BIG OLD F...
BLAZE
BLAZE
BLAZE
SQUIK SQUEAK

WHILE LLOYD MAY HAVE FAILED THE COMBAT TEST...
RETURN THE WEAPON HERE.
OH RIGHT.
I BROUGHT A NEW DUMMY!
...THE WRITTEN TEST AND INTERVIEW WOULD DECIDE HIS FATE.

THOSE HE'D MET ALONG THE WAY EXPECTED GREAT THINGS...
THE BOY HEADED TO THE NEXT TESTING LOCATION, HIS FACE GRIM.
to be continued...
OH!
CLINK
IT'S GETTING DARK OUT.
I WONDER IF IT'S GOING TO RAIN.

I HOPE LLOYD'S NERVES DON'T GET THE BEST OF HIM.
SIP
THE CROWD MUST BE HUGE!

HE MUST'VE SEEN THAT STATUE ...

WHAT A GREAT STATUE!
CITIES ARE AMAZING!
I CAN TOTALLY SEE HIM SAYING THAT.
HEH HEH...

BUT THAT STATUE'S JUST A VAIN LIE.
PLIP
THE REAL KING'S OLD AND CHUBBY!
YES, THE REAL...
PLIP
PLIP
......

DAD...
SHAAAA
PTAPTAP...

WRITTEN
TEST

Suppose
a Kid from the
LAST DUNGEON
BOONIES Moved
to a
Starter Town

LLOYD DID QUITE POORLY IN THE COMBAT TEST...
...FAILING UTTERLY TO COMMUNICATE HIS STRENGTH.

THE WRITTEN TEST ASKED ABOUT MAGICAL KNOWLEDGE...
...AND THE INTERVIEW DEMANDED THE RECRUITS PITCH THEMSELVES VERBALLY.

WHITHER LIES YOUNG LLOYD'S FATE?!
AH...
AUGH...
YES! I PASSED!

BWAH HA HA!
THIS WAS EASY FOR ME!
YOU SAID IT!
OH, THANK GOODNESS! I FOUND MY NAME!
CHATTER
WHOOOO!
AH, DAMN. GUESS I'M STUCK RUNNING THE FAMILY BUSINESS.
OH NO...
MY NAME ...
...ISN'T THERE.
THOSE WHO PASSED PROCEED TO ORIENTATION.
COME INSIDE.
YEAH!
OH NO...
......
CHATTER
THE RESULTS HAVE BEEN POSTED...

IS THAT REALLY TRUE?
IT IS!
MY DAUGHTER WORKS IN THE CASTLE.
SHE SAYS THE BIGWIGS ARE ALL ARGUING ABOUT WAR PREPARATIONS.
......!

YOU'VE HEARD THE RUMORS, RIGHT?
THEY SAY THE JIOU EMPIRE BLEW UP A ROAD, CAUSING A ROCKSLIDE... EVEN BLOCKED A RIVER.
THE BIGWIGS THOUGHT WE WERE ON THE BRINK OF WAR!
BUT FOR SOME REASON, THOSE PROB-LEMS SUD-DENLY WENT AWAY!
AND NOW, THEY'RE BUTTING HEADS OVER WHETHER OR NOT JIOU WAS TO BLAME, PUTTING THE WAR PREP ON HOLD.
I MOVED SOME ROCKS!
I MADE IT RAIN AND FILLED THE RIVER!
BUT WE WERE THAT CLOSE TO WAR?
THESE INCIDENTS DEFINITELY WEREN'T A COINCIDENCE.
AND THERE ARE THE MONSTERS TOO... IF SOMEONE BEHIND THE SCENES IS TRYING TO INCITE WAR...
KNOWS EXACTLY WHY
I WONDER WHY...
OH, OW! MY ELBOW ...!
AHHH.
HERE, YOUR MEDICINE'S READY.

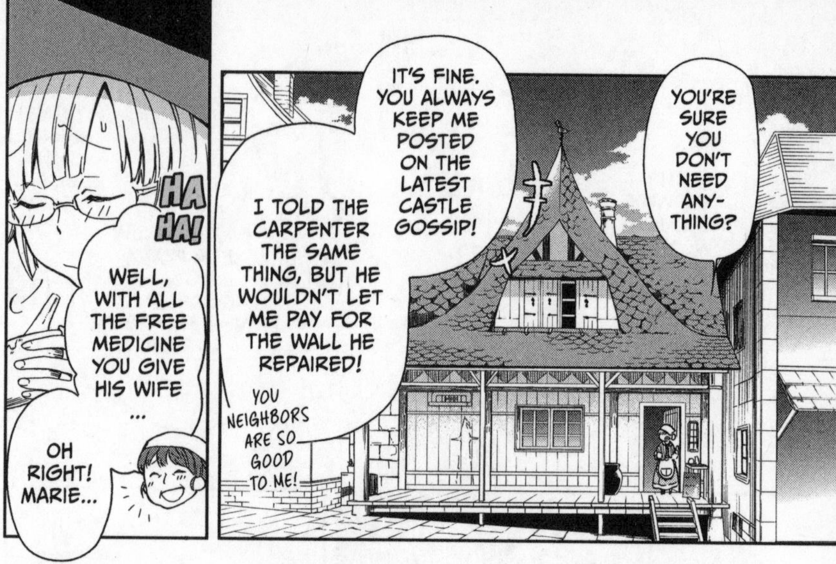
YOU'RE SURE YOU DON'T NEED ANY-THING?
IT'S FINE. YOU ALWAYS KEEP ME POSTED ON THE LATEST CASTLE GOSSIP!
I TOLD THE CARPENTER THE SAME THING, BUT HE WOULDN'T LET ME PAY FOR THE WALL HE REPAIRED!
YOU NEIGHBORS ARE SO GOOD TO ME!
HA HA!
WELL, WITH ALL THE FREE MEDICINE YOU GIVE HIS WIFE ...
OH RIGHT! MARIE...

YOU HAVEN'T COME OVER FOR DINNER LATELY...
I HEAR YOU'VE GOT YOUR NEW BOY TOY COOKING FOR YOU?
CRASH

YOU USUALLY LIVE ON CANNED FOOD...
...AND GET SO SICK OF IT, YOU COME BEGGING FOR HOME-COOKED MEALS.
GOT ANYTHING TO SPARE?
BACK AGAIN, HUH?
AND THEY SAY YOU TWO SEEM VERY CLOSE.
SPROING
N-N-NOT LIKE THAT!

HE'S A RELA-TIVE'S...
I MEAN, I'M A WITCH! OF COURSE, I HAVE A MINION!
IS THAT WHAT THEY CALL IT THESE DAYS?
YOU CERTAINLY DO DOTE ON THIS "MINION."
WHAT?! I'M SUPER-STRICT, I'LL HAVE YOU KNOW!

AH HA HA!
SHE'S FINALLY GONE... UGH, I JUST FANNED THE RUMOR FLAMES, DIDN'T I?
HFF! HFF!
BETTER MAKE SOME COFFEE AND CALM DOWN.

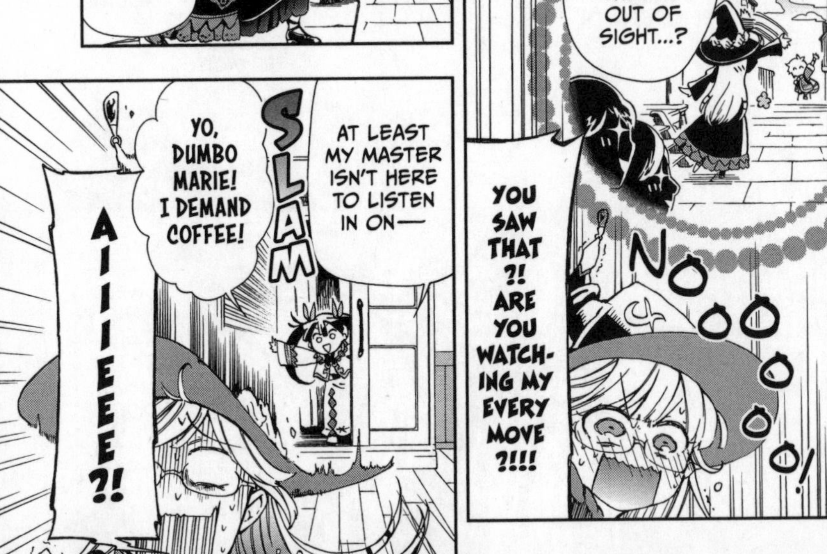
DO TODAY'S WITCHES FIX THEIR MINIONS' BED HEADS?
THEN STAND AT THE DOOR WAVING AFTER THEM TILL THEY'RE OUT OF SIGHT...?
NOOOOOOO!
YOU SAW THAT?! ARE YOU WATCHING MY EVERY MOVE?!!!
AT LEAST MY MASTER ISN'T HERE TO LISTEN IN ON—
SLAM
YO, DUMBO MARIE! I DEMAND COFFEE!
AIIIEEE?!

EEEP!!
WHY ARE YOU HERE THIS TIME?
TEST RESULTS ARE UP, RIGHT?
HE'LL PASS! WE'LL CELEBRATE! I'LL STEAL A SMOOCH!
HAVE YOU NO SENSE OF SHAME?!!
YOU HAD COMPANY?
I WAS GATHERING INTEL.
THIS SHOP TRADES IN ALL KINDS OF THINGS.
FROM WHAT I LEARNED TODAY...
...CERTAIN FORCES ARE CONSPIRING TO INCITE WAR.
THE THREAT IS GETTING SERIOUS.
OH HOH?
WELL, HANG IN THERE.
THE FASTER YOU'RE BACK IN THE PALACE, THE BETTER, MARIE!
JOLT
OR SHOULD I SAY...

CASE 4
This Shock Was Like Seeing a Jewel That Could Save the Realm's Economy Flung into the Ocean
...THE MISSING MEMBER OF THE AZAMI ROYAL FAMILY...
... PRINCESS MARIA?!
THE WITCH OF THE EAST SIDE AKA. THE AZAMI PRINCESS MARIA AZAMI
EVEN IF LLOYD DOES FAIL HIS TEST...
...YOU CAN SET THINGS RIGHT, PROVIDED YOU RECLAIM YOUR AUTHORITY.

......
THAT
WHAT THE HECK KINDA POSE IS THAT?
YOU... LO...... GRA...

IS THAT WHY YOU SENT LLOYD TO ME?!
YOWL
WELL, YEAH.
NOD

LLOYD'S A GOOD KID. HOW CAN YOU NOT WANT TO LOOK AFTER HIM?
JUST... DON'T GET TOO CLOSE.
IF I SEE ANY ROMANCE BREWING, I'LL...
FLINCH
NO! WAIT, BACK UP!

I CAN'T GO BACK TO THE PALACE YET!
NOT UNTIL I FIGURE OUT WHO'S TRYING TO START THIS WAR!
ROCKSLIDES ON THE ROADS, RIVERS DRYING UP, MONSTERS INCREASING...
SOMEONE'S DOING ALL THAT TO FAN RESENTMENT OF THE JIOU EMPIRE.

I'M TOLD THE KING... THAT IS, MY FATHER...IS BEDRIDDEN. HE'S SERIOUSLY ILL.
THE CURSE THIS VILLAIN PLACED ON HIM MUST HAVE TAKEN ITS TOLL.
IT'S BEEN FIVE YEARS SINCE HE WAS TRANSFORMED INTO A WAR-MONGER...

HA HA...
I DON'T SUPPOSE YOU COULD SAVE US, HUH?
THAT'D BE SO EASY.
MARIE... I'VE TOLD YOU THIS BEFORE.

KUNLUN VILLAGERS CAN ONLY HELP WITH TWO THINGS.
DEMON LORDS...
...AND DISASTERS.
ONLY MATTERS BEYOND HUMAN COMPREHENSION... WE CAN'T INVOLVE OURSELVES IN POWER STRUGGLES BETWEEN HUMANS.
HUMANS NEED TO MAKE MISTAKES.
THEY GROW BY LEARNING FROM THEM...
...OR DESTROY THEMSELVES IN THE PROCESS.
......
I KNOW AS MUCH. THAT'S WHY I WAS SO DESPERATE...
...TO LEARN THE DISENCHANT RUNE FROM YOU.
THEN, GOOD.

SO? ANYTHING ELSE TO REPORT?
NO... HONESTLY, I CAN'T BEGIN TO TELL WHO'S ON WHAT SIDE.
I BET THERE'S EVEN GOOD GUYS WHO DON'T REALIZE THEY'RE WORKING FOR EVIL.

JUST DON'T GET LLOYD MIXED UP IN THIS.
ANYTHING WEIRD HAPPENING ON THAT FRONT?
WITH LLOYD ...?
OTHER THAN HOW STRONG HE...?
UH, LEMME SEE...

HE'S BEEN OUT OF SORTS SINCE THE EXAM.
THE BOY NEVER HAS HAD ANY CON-FIDENCE.
AND, UH... OH!
A BEAUTIFUL GIRL'S BEEN GOING AROUND LOOKING FOR HIM.
SHE SAYS FATE BROUGHT THEM TOGETHER.

SO THE REASON LLOYD'S DOWN...
...IS HEART-BREAK?!!
THAT'S... QUITE A JUMP.
RIGHT! I'LL JUST DESTROY THIS REALM!!
STOP! DON'T BE STUPID, MASTER!!
YOU CAN'T LEVEL COUNTRIES EVERY TIME YOU GET MAD!
LIKE THAT TIME YOUR PARFAIT HAD FEWER STRAW-BERRIES THAN THE PICTURE!
OHHH, WHY DID YOU REMIND ME?!
NOW I HAVE TO LEVEL IT TWICE!!
DON'T DO IT, LOLI GRAND-MAAA!!!
WHILE MARIE WAS BUSY SAVING THE KINGDOM FROM CERTAIN DOOM...

...THE NEW CADETS, FRESH FROM PASSING THE EXAM, HAD GATHERED IN A LECTURE HALL.
GOOD, GOOD.
LOTS OF POTENTIAL MARKS MADE IT THROUGH.
OH! THE BELT PRINCESS ...

OH... SHE'S LOOKING FOR THAT BOY OF HERS.
LLOYD ...?
GLANCE GLANCE

LLOYD WOULD MAKE ANY JOB EASIER...
IF I RIDE HIS COATTAILS, MY WALLET WILL FILL RIGHT UP.
......
HMM?

WHIP!!
WHIP
WHAP
YOU'RE KIDDING ?!
HE FAILED ?!
RIHO FLAVIN ...?
STEP

OH GOOD! LLO—
THE ONE-ARMED MERCE-NARY!
THEY TOOK YOU FOR REAL?
WELL, HERE'S HOPI—
TCH!

NOT NOW.
WHAAAAAAAAAAT?
CLANK

H—
HOW COULD ANYONE TREAT ME LIKE...
!

YO, BELT—
FWSH
GLANCE TIME: 0.0002 SECONDS
NOT NOW.
WHAT IS THIS? HOW COULD HE HAVE FAILED?!
WHY NOT NOW?
DEFLATED
OKAY, TAKE YOUR SEATS!
CON-GRATS ON PASSING!
TIME FOR ORIEN-TATION.
MERTHO-PHAN!
HE SEEMS CALM... DOES HE KNOW WHY LLOYD ISN'T HERE?

FIRST, ROLL CALL...
WHAT'S UP, MERTHO-PHAN?
CALL THEIR NAMES.
LOOK
UH... ANYBODY LATE?
IN THE BATH-ROOM ...?
LOOK
HE JUST NOTICED ...?! THEY SERIOUSLY CUT LLOYD?!
IS THIS ALL OF YOU ?!

RIGHT!
ANYONE NOT HERE, RAISE YOUR HAND!!
C'MON !!
MERTHO-PHAN! DIGNITY! AUTHOR-ITY!!
I GET IT, BUT... GEEZ, MAN...
UM, EXCUSE ME!

IS THAT YOU, LLO —?!
DID LLOYD SOMEHOW NOT PASS?
OR NOT...
AHEM, BELT PRIN-CESS!
NOT THE TIME FOR PERSONAL QUESTIONS!

CAREFUL! YOU DON'T WANT MERTHO-PHAN MAD AT—
BAM
TOSS
TAKE OVER, CHOLINE.
HUH?!
I THOUGHT THE SAME THING!!
WHAT HAPPENED TO YOUR STONY EXPRES-SION?!
I'M GONNA INTERRO-GATE THE INTER-VIEWERS.
FOR A BOY LIKE THAT TO FAIL THE EXAM...
...SOME-THING MUST HAVE GONE WRONG!!!
I'M COMING TOO!
MIND IF I JOIN YOU?
DOINK
GLAD TO HAVE YOU!
NEED INTEL ON LLOYD!
CADETS! YOU'LL MISS ORIEN-TATION!

SLAM
EEP!

I UNDERSTAND YOU WERE THE ONE TO INTERVIEW LLOYD BELLADONNA.
EEEK!
I'LL GET RIGHT TO THE POINT.
WHY DID YOU FAIL HIM?
ER, WELL... YOU SEE...
EEEK! THIS IS TERRI-FYING!
NOD NOD
NOBODY WANTS TO SEE THIS...
I AIN'T STOPPING HIM, THOUGH.
H—
HE JUST STARTED BABBLING NONSENSE!
ABOUT HIS LOVE FOR ME ...?!
CAN IT, BELT PRIN-CESS!
NONSENSE?
GLARE

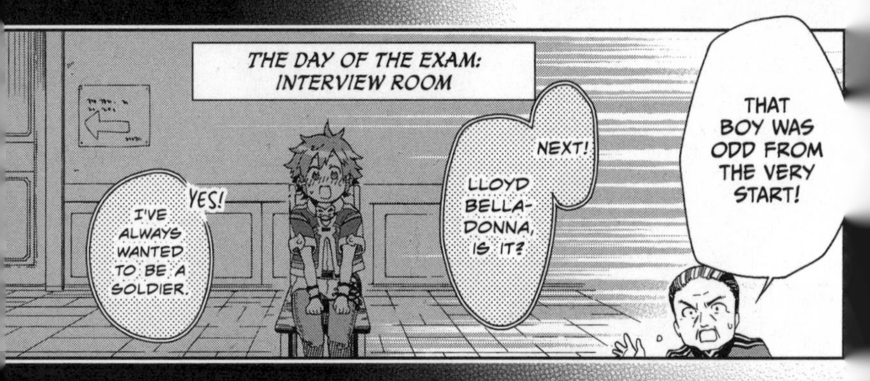
THAT BOY WAS ODD FROM THE VERY START!
THE DAY OF THE EXAM: INTERVIEW ROOM
NEXT!
LLOYD BELLADONNA, IS IT?
YES!
I'VE ALWAYS WANTED TO BE A SOLDIER.

I SEE, AND YOU'RE FROM...
KUNLUN...?
YOU'RE SWEATING A LOT, SON.
I'M FINE!
NEVER HEARD OF IT. WHERE IS IT, EXACTLY?
THE FAR EDGE OF THE CONTINENT.
YOU DON'T SAY?

LOOK, HE'S JUST A HICK FROM THE BOONIES.
YEAH, I CAN SEE THAT.
RIGHT! ANYTHING YOU'RE PARTICULARLY GOOD AT?
UHM...
COOKING, LAUNDRY...
CLEANING...
WE'RE NOT HIRING SERVANTS!
JOLT
SORRY! UH, WELL, THERE IS MAGIC...
MAGIC...?!

I CAN MAKE RAIN!
RAIN?
WE THOUGHT HE WAS NUTS.
TAK TAK TAK
LET ME JUST SHOW YOU.
WHAT? DON'T...
SCRITCH SCRATCH

WHOOSH

IT SHOULD START RAINING IN A FEW MINUTES.
SURE IT WILL.
THAT'S ENOUGH. YOU CAN GO.
OH... OKAY.

RAIN! WHAT A RIDICULOUS LIE.
BUT IT DID ACTUALLY RAIN THAT DAY.

COUNTRY FOLK KNOW HOW TO READ THE SKIES AND PREDICT THE WEATHER!
THAT'S ALL HE DID! THEN HE LIED ABOUT MAKING IT RAIN BY HIMSELF!
※ACTUALLY USED ANCIENT RUNE RAIN MAGIC
IF HE REALLY COULD, THAT WOULD BE HUGE...
IT WAS HUGE.
AND ON TOP OF THAT...!
SP-I-N
BAM
LOOM
HE FILLED HIS WRITTEN TEST WITH MEANINGLESS DOODLES!
?!
THE ARMY DOESN'T NEED HIM.
SERIOUSLY, IS ANYONE ENJOYING THIS?
MAYBE YOU SHOULD SHUT UP.
BUT THAT BOY WAS SO...
I'LL FETCH HIS ANSWER SHEET FOR YOU.
SEE FOR YOURSELF.

DOO-DLES...
NO OTHER WORD FOR IT.
HEY! MER-THO-PHAN...!!
SLAM

STOMP
STOMP
STOMP
YOU DUMPED ALL YOUR WORK ON ME?!
HNGH! SORRY!
SLAP
YOU'RE BUYING ME A PARFAIT THIS WEEK-END!

SO ...?
WHAT'S THE STORY WITH THIS LLOYD KID?
YOU THREE IDIOTS SATISFIED?
!

SHOVE
HE'S SUCH A CREATIVE SOUL, THE ANSWER SHEET COULDN'T CONTAIN HIM!
COLONEL CHOLINE, SHE'S THE ONLY IDIOT HERE.
WHAT, IS THAT HIS ANSWER SHEET?
SHOVE
SHOOOVE

......
HONESTLY, THE INTERVIEWER MADE THE RIGHT CALL.
WE'LL HAVE TO FIND SOME OTHER WAY FOR HIM TO JOIN OUR RANKS.
HANG ON.
I KNOW! I'M GOING TOO FAR, BUT FOR THE REALM—
NO, SHUT UP! WHAT THE HELL?!!
THESE ARE ANCIENT RUNES!!
ANCIENT ...?
RUNES ...?

RUNES ARE A FORM OF MAGIC USED IN ANCIENT CIVILIZA-TIONS.
THEY WERE LOST LONG AGO AND ARE THE SUBJECT OF MUCH RESEARCH, MY OWN INCLUDED.

OH?
SO THESE ARE RUNES?
DONK
YOU ORDERED ME TO RESEARCH 'EM...
..."FOR THE SAKE OF THE REALM!" AND NOW YOU'RE SHOCKED?!
ARGH!
S...SORRY.
SO WHAT'RE THEY GOOD FOR?
BESIDES BEING OLD...

CURIOUS? WELL, NORMALLY, MAGIC IS DONE WITH CHANTS OR BY USING STAFFS AND JEWELS AS CONDUITS, BUT THESE...
BLAH!
BLAH!
SORRY. CAN YOU CUT TO THE CHASE?
UGH.
THEY'RE ANCIENT SUPER-MAGIC.
THANKS!
THAT MIGHT BE TOO SIMPLE.

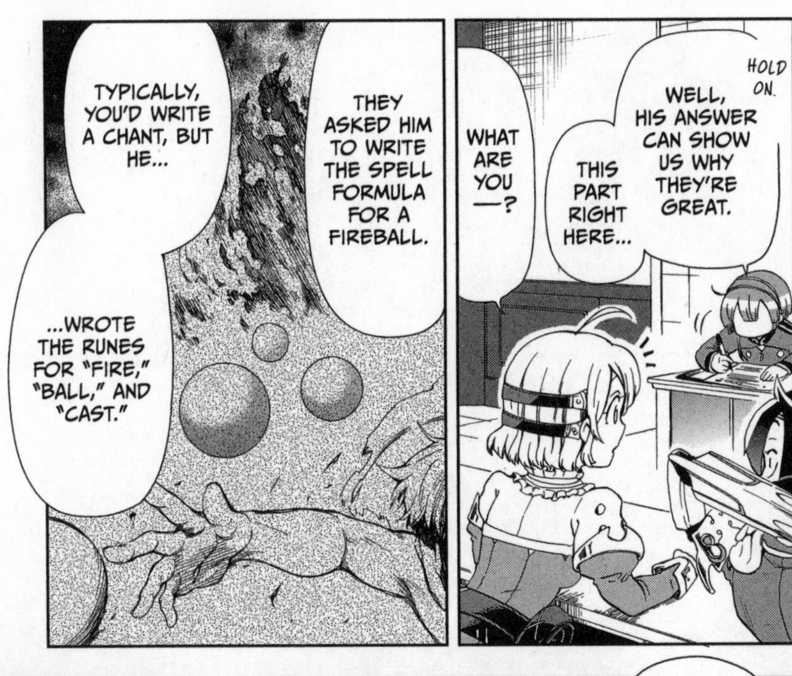
HOLD ON.
WELL, HIS ANSWER CAN SHOW US WHY THEY'RE GREAT.
THIS PART RIGHT HERE...
WHAT ARE YOU—?
THEY ASKED HIM TO WRITE THE SPELL FORMULA FOR A FIREBALL.
TYPICALLY, YOU'D WRITE A CHANT, BUT HE...
...WROTE THE RUNES FOR "FIRE," "BALL," AND "CAST."

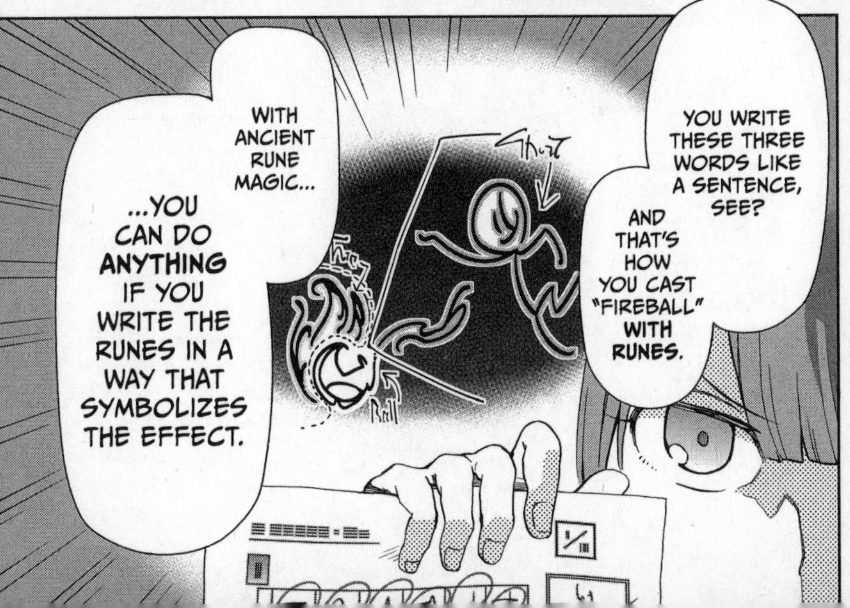
YOU WRITE THESE THREE WORDS LIKE A SENTENCE, SEE?
AND THAT'S HOW YOU CAST "FIREBALL" WITH RUNES.
WITH ANCIENT RUNE MAGIC...
...YOU CAN DO ANYTHING IF YOU WRITE THE RUNES IN A WAY THAT SYMBOLIZES THE EFFECT.

IS THAT WHY THEY LOOK LIKE DOODLES?
I ONLY KNOW THE RUNE FOR "CAST," SO THE REST IS A GUESS.
BUT THE KEY IS THE FEEL OF IT.
NORMAL MAGIC USES PREEXISTING CHANTS OR SIGILS AIMING FOR A FIXED OUTCOME.
WITH RUNES, YOU CAN CREATE SPELLS AS LONG AS YOU HAVE THE MAGIC FOR IT!!
FOR EXAMPLE, IF YOU TAKE THE RUNES FOR "WORLD," "DESTROY," "DRAGON," AND "SUMMON"...
...AND WRITE THEM OUT SO IT FEELS LIKE SUMMONING A WORLD-DESTROYING DRAGON...
...YOU COULD ACTUALLY SUMMON A FEAR-SOME DRAGON THAT WOULD DESTROY THE WORLD!!

IF YOU HAVE MAGIC STRONG ENOUGH TO DO THAT, DO YOU REALLY NEED THE RUNES?
JUST AN EXAMPLE! IF ANYONE WAS THAT STRONG, THE WORLD WOULD BE LONG GONE.
MEAN-WHILE, OVER AT MARIE'S SHOP
IF LLOYD ISN'T MINE, THIS WORLD MUST END!
"WORLD," "DESTROY," "DRAGON," AND...
DON'T USE RUNES FOR THAT!!
IT'S EVIL!
SO YOU NEED THE WORDS, SKILL, AND RAW MAGIC POWER TO USE RUNES...
...BUT YOU CAN DO THINGS WITH 'EM MODERN MAGIC CAN ONLY DREAM OF.
BUT THEY AIN'T EFFICIENT, BURN MAGIC LIKE CRAZY, AND USING NORMAL MAGIC IS WAY EASIER.
CAN YOU USE THEM, COLONEL CHOLINE?
A LITTLE... IT TAKES AGES, AND MY SUCCESS RATE'S NOT GREAT.
LIKE, WE FOUND A RUNE THAT CAN MAKE A METEOR FALL...
BUT NOBODY HAS ENOUGH MAGIC TO PULL IT OFF. ALL THAT RESEARCH IN VAIN!
SLUMP
THAT'S ODD...

WHY BRING THEM BACK IF YOU CAN'T USE THEM?
THEY SOUND EITHER IMPRACTICAL OR IMPOSSIBLE!
PURE COOL FACTOR ...?

BUT YOU SAID IT WAS "FOR THE REALM."
YOU MUST HAVE HAD SOMEONE...
UH... WELL, WE DID...
SHE'S RIGHT.
CLNK...

WE HAD SOMEONE WITH THE CAPACITY ...
...FOR THE MOST POWERFUL MAGIC IN THE KINGDOM ...

THE MISSING PRINCESS ...
...MARIA AZAMI HERSELF!
AAAAH! AAAAAH!
AHCHOOO!
SPLOOSH
AUGH! ROYAL GERMS IN MY EYES!!
S-SORRY! SOMEONE MUST BE GOSSIPING...

MARIA'S MAGIC POTENTIAL IS INCREDIBLE.
SHE COULD EASILY MASTER ANCIENT RUNES...
...AND THAT WOULD BE DECISIVE IN A WAR AGAINST THE JIOU EMPIRE...
...WHICH WAS WHY WE STUDIED THE METEOR RUNE.

I AIN'T SO SURE SHE'D AGREE...
...TO LEARN A SPELL THAT NASTY, WAR OR NO WAR.
FOR THE SAKE OF THE REALM... I'M SURE...
HMM?

WITH HER DIS-APPEAR-ANCE, PLANS STALLED...
WHERE COULD SHE BE?
SHE'S IN AZAMI, ON THE EAST SIDE...
I'M DIS-INFECTING THE ENTIRE WORLD!!
STOPPPP!
MUTTER
NO, WE'D MAKE HER AGREE.
OH, THE PRINCESS THING REMINDS ME...
PAT

YOU EACH GET ONE TOO.
FWAP
A SEARCH ORDER FOR THE PRINCESS?
IS THIS GIRL HER?

YEAH, WELL... FROM FIVE YEARS AGO.
WE HAND THESE OUT AT ORIEN-TATION EVERY YEAR.

NOT JUST MONEY? A PROMOTION, AND ANY REQUESTS WITHIN REASON?!
DAMN! NOW THAT'S A REWARD!
THE ARMY HAS BEEN SEARCHING FOR HER WITH NO RESULTS.

OUR SUPERIORS ARE HOPING NUMBERS WILL HELP...
FOOLS.
AND YOU DON'T APPROVE, COLONEL?

WITH THE FOUNDATION DAY FESTIVAL AROUND THE CORNER, WE NEED TO WHIP THE RECRUITS INTO SHAPE!
BUT EVERY YEAR, WE GET IDIOTS AFTER THE REWARD CAUSING TROUBLE.
AND I HAVE TO WIPE THEIR BUTTS FOR THEM.
ROOOAR
THEY WERE FIRED UP AGAIN THIS YEAR!
ESPECIALLY THAT ALLAN CHARACTER ...
AT ORIENTATION

THROWING CADETS AT IT WON'T MAKE ANY DIFFER-ENCE.
DON'T YOU PAY IT ANY ATTENTION.
IF WE FIND THE PRINCESS, CAN WE GET LLOYD ENLISTED?
COLONEL CHOLINE, HOW FAR DOES THIS REWARD STRETCH?
PLEASE, JUST... DON'T SCREW UP!

MWAH HA HA HA!
PRETTY PLEEEASE ...?
AWW, LET 'EM HAVE THEIR FUN!
SLUMP
THEY FIND THE PRIN-CESS, THEY'LL BE SET.
AND WE CAN FINALLY TRY THAT METEOR RUNE OUT.
...
HAAAH...
DIDN'T THINK IT WOULD TAKE SO MUCH TIME...

THERE'S SO MANY OTHER RUNES WE COULD'VE STARTED WITH.
RUNES TO MAKE FLOWERS BLOOM OR MAKE IT RAIN...
RAIN ...?!!
YEAH, WE FOUND ONE THAT MIGHT DO THAT.
WHY ARE THERE ANCIENT RUNES ON THIS ANSWER SHEET ANYWAY?
COLONEL MERTHO-PHAN...
IF LLOYD CAN MAKE IT RAIN, DOES HE PASS?
HMM... BUT...
..."THESE ARE ANCIENT RUNES" JUST WON'T CUT IT.
IT'D BE HARD TO OVERTURN THE DECISION FOR SUCH A PECULIAR REASON.
THAT INTER-VIEWER WON'T BELIEVE IT, NO...
HNNNGH...
BUT ...!
IF HE IS THE REAL DEAL, WE CAN'T LET HIM GO.
......

HE'S A BONAFIDE OUT-OF-PLACE ARTIFACT! A SHAMAN WHO CAN MAKE IT RAIN? HE'D RAKE IT IN!
LLOYD BELLA-DONNA... WITH HIM, THE REALM'S MILITARY POWER WOULD BE SECURED...
OH, LLOYD... YOU WANTED TO MARRY ME SO MUCH, YOU EVEN USED RUNES TO HELP YOU ENLIST!
MUTTER
MUTTER
MUTTER
MUTTER
MUTTER
MUTTER
SO...
... WHERE IS THE APPLI-CANT WHO WROTE THIS?
BWAH! HA! HA! HA! HA! HA! HEH! HEH! HEH! HEH!

YOU AIN'T GONNA TELL ME HE FAILED AND WENT BACK HOME, RIGHT?
THERE'S NO WAY... HA! HA! HA! HA!
TAK
TAK
TAK
TAK
TAK
SHP!!
I GUESS WE CAN TAKE THESE DOWN?
YEAH, EVERY-ONE'S GONE.
WHOOSH

WHERE ARE YOU, LLOYD BELLA-DONNA-AAAAA-AAA?!!!
LLOYD, I'M RIGHT HEEERE!
YIKES, KNOCK THAT OFF!
CRINGE
UH, SORRY... I DON'T KNOW THESE IDIOTS.
DON'T LOOK AT ME LIKE THAT!

LLOYD! LLOYD! LLOYD! LLOYD!
UGH.
I HOPE LLOYD GETS HOME SOON...
HE'S LATE...

SUPPOSE A KID FROM THE LAST DUNGEON BOONIES MOVED TO A STARTER TOWN 1 ~ THE END

TRANSLATION NOTES

Page 6
Belladonna: Italian for "beautiful woman," Lloyd's surname is also the name for a medicinal plant known as deadly nightshade, which can be fatal to humans if consumed.

Page 16
Alka: This name appears to be derived from "alkaline," an adjective used to describe substances with a basic pH (as opposed to acidic) and which can also be found in the brand name of a certain fizzy antacid, as well as alkaline batteries.

Page 65
Jiou Empire: Jiou is an herb used in traditional Chinese medicine. Its scientific name is *Rehmannia glutinosa*.

Page 72
Selen: This name possibly comes from the word "selenium," which itself is derived from the Ancient Greek for "moon." Selenium is an element used in glassmaking and pigments.

Page 108
Allan Toin Lidocaine: Allantoin is a naturally occurring chemical compound that promotes healing, while lidocaine is a local anesthetic.

Page 122
Merthophan Dextro: This instructor's name is a play on dextromethorphan, a medication used in many cold and cough medicines.

Page 122
Choline Sterase: Another name with its roots in biochemistry, this comes from cholinesterase, a name for a family of enzymes that are necessary for proper nervous system function in the human body.

Page 126
Riho Flavin: The mercenary's name is a play on riboflavin, which is better known as vitamin B_2 and can be found in various foods and supplements.

Page 161
Maria Azami: This is the Japanese name for the milk thistle or Marian thistle, *azami* being the Japanese word for "thistle."

BONUS LAST DUNGEON KID

LLOYD AND SELEN
~THE NIGHT BEFORE RESULTS~

OH LLOYD!
I COULDN'T TRACK DOWN YOUR ABODE.

BUT WE'LL MEET AT THE RESULTS POSTING!
I SIMPLY MUST LOOK PERFECT!
RUMMAGE RUMMAGE
...!!

I HAVE NOTHING TO WEAR!
NOTHING NICE! MINIMAL FUNCTIONAL GEAR FOR TRAVELING!
WOOL UNDERWEAR!
I HAVE TO BUY SOMETHING TONIGHT!

BRIDAL GOWN SHOPS?

THEY'D BE CLOSED BY NOW...

THIS IS AN EMERGENCY.

THROB THROB

EEK ...

← INNKEEPER

GIRLS IN LOVE ARE ALWAYS FULL THROTTLE.

LLOYD AND RIHO
~WHERE IS HE NOW?~

SO LLOYD CAN USE RUNES, HUH?
I CAN JUST SMELL THE MOOLAH!!

BUT WHO IS HE, REALLY?
BLAH! BLAH! BLAH! BLAH!
TAKES A LOT OF MAGIC TO MAKE IT RAIN...

IS HE REALLY A HUNDRED-YEAR-OLD WIZARD? NO WAY!
BUT HIS STRENGTH IS LIKE A LEGENDARY HERO'S...

I'M COMING, MY DEAR LLOYD!
DASH
WAIT! BELLADONNA!

QUITE THE MENTAL IMAGE

Special Thanks

Original Work: Toshio Satou
Character Design: Nao Watanuki
GA Bunko Side Editors/Staff
Thank you for all your help!

Manga Editors
I-ta and **F**-moto
Assistant: Yoshichika Eguchi
Also, thanks to everyone who helped with printing/design/etc.

and You

Thank you for reading!
✿ SEE YOU NEXT TIME! ✿

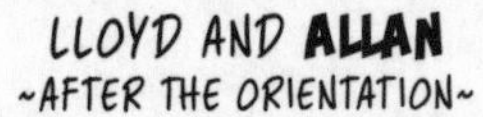

EASILY PASSED THE TEST!
PROMOTION LIES AHEAD!

OH, THAT'S ALLAN.
LIDOCAINE? I HEAR HE'S CRAZY STRONG!
HEH HEH HEH!

HE CHOPPED UP THAT DUMMY IN THE COMBAT TEST.
IMPRESSIVE.
......
NO...
HE PULVERIZED IT IN A SINGLE BLOW!

EXPECTA-TIONS ARE A HEAVY BURDEN.
HOW DID THIS HAPPEN?
?
CAUSE
I FAILED

RUMORS ALWAYS GET EMBELLISHED

UP NEXT
LLOYD FAILED AND IS DEPRESSED...
HA HA HA...
REALLY?
NOW WHAT?
BUT A NEW ENCOUNTER...
MAYBE TOMORROW.
WHO'S THERE ?!
HUH?
NONE OF YOUR BUSINESS...
THIS IS MY HEART'S DESIRE.
AH.
DEFINITELY SOMETHING DUMB.
LLOYD'S INHUMAN FATE TAKES HIM TO ...!?
Suppose a Kid from the LAST DUNGEON BOONIES Moved to a Starter Town
VOLUME 2, COMING SOON!

Special Comment

CONGRATULATIONS ON THE RELEASE OF VOLUME 1! I'M LOOKING FORWARD TO FUSEMACHI'S VERSION OF MY CHARACTERS EVERY TIME! THEY'RE ALL SO ADORABLE! I CAN'T WAIT FOR MORE!

TOSHIO SATOU

HIS CAREFUL DEPICTIONS OF MY TIME-CONSUMING DESIGNS MADE ME VERY HAPPY. I LEARNED FROM THE DETAIL AND ENERGY OF THE MANGA ART, AND I'M PUTTING THAT ALL INTO THE NOVEL ILLUSTRATIONS!

NAO WATANUKI

CONGRATS!
MANGA VOL. 1
RELEASE!!

Suppose a Kid from the Last Dungeon Boonies Moved to a Starter Town 1

STORY BY
TOSHIO SATOU

ART BY
HAJIME FUSEMACHI

CHARACTER DESIGN BY
NAO WATANUKI

Translation: Andrew Cunningham
Lettering: Rochelle Gancio
Logo Design: Wendy Chan
Cover Design: Abigail Blackman
Editor: Tania Biswas

ISBN: 978-1-64609-037-2

Library of Congress Cataloging-in-Publication Data is on file with the publisher.

Printed in the U.S.A.
First printing, March 2020
10 9 8 7 6 5 4 3 2 1

SQUARE ENIX
MANGA & BOOKS
www.square-enix-books.com